IN
PRAISE
OF
SIMPLE
THINGS

IN PRAISE OF SIMPLE THINGS

Greer &
Melvin
Fitting

DAVID McKAY COMPANY
New York

IN PRAISE OF SIMPLE THINGS

Library of Congress Cataloging in Publication Data

Fitting, Greer.
    In praise of simple things.

    Bibliography: p.
    Includes index.
    1. Agriculture—Handbooks, manuals, etc. 2. Farm life.
3. Canning and preserving. 3. Wine and wine making.
I. Fitting, Melvin, joint author. II. Title.
S501.2.F57   640   75–19051
ISBN 0–679–50511–3

MANUFACTURED IN THE UNITED STATES OF AMERICA

Designed by Bob Antler

This book is dedicated to
Helen and Chris Fitting
and to their granddaughters
Miriam Amy Fitting and
Rebecca Jo Fitting

OUR
THANKS
TO:

First and foremost, Helen and Chris Fitting, Mel's parents, who made it possible for us to move to the country, and who taught us many of the skills which keep us warm and happy. Also we want to thank many of their friends who helped us with advice, know-how, chicken feeders, garden plants, etc., especially Alda and Merrill French.

We heartily thank Oscar Collier, Greer's father, whose idea it was that we write this book, and who encouraged us at every stage of its writing.

Our thanks to Eleanor Rawson, formerly of David McKay Company, Inc., for her enthusiasm about the project, and for many of her helpful suggestions.

We particularly want to thank Sandy Gutkaiss who lives down the road, and who cheerfully performed many of the necessary but not very exciting clerical tasks connected with this book.

And of course there is Miriam, who was so patient during all those hours when Mommy and Daddy were busy working. She never once upset any of the piles and piles of papers which represented the various stages of this book.

CONTENTS

INTRODUCTION

Three years ago we moved from New York City to the country. Since then, we've acquired many skills ranging from chicken raising to winemaking. This book is an account of what we've found out, and how we found it out.

We've each become knowledgeable about different things, so each of us separately has written appropriate chapters. Thus Greer discusses gardening and Mel discusses winemaking. The book has two voices as well as two authors. It makes more sense that way.

In our life in the country, we are aiming at self-sufficiency. Homesteading, in other words. But what we have to say may be of use to you even if you aren't willing to go to such an extreme. Gardening can be done in any backyard, and winemaking in any apartment. And if you do want to homestead, maybe our account will give you some idea of what is in store.

So, there you have it. Stated most simply, this book is a biography of us and our cabbages. We hope you enjoy it.

CHAPTER 1

HOW
TO BRING
A HOUSE
UP RIGHT

Melvin speaking

Putting the House in Its Place

For years before we bought it, our house had been going downhill. Literally. Some kids who used to live in our house told us that on rainy Saturdays they used to coast down the kitchen floor in toy cars. To be precise, the kitchen floor sloped with a drop of half a foot or more from front to back. (The bathroom would have been the same, but it had been "fixed" by the building of a level false floor.) The rest of the downstairs was not affected. Now the real problem, it was clear, wasn't the floor, but the foundation. We could tell

1

because the second story had a slope comparable to the one in the kitchen floor, and the roof took quite a dip at just that point. The house had been built in sections, each with its own foundation. That is why most of the house could be fundamentally sound even though part of it was badly damaged.

When we bought the house we knew there was a problem. That was obvious. It also seemed clear the problem was serious and involved the foundation. How serious it was we didn't know; that part of the house was covered with tar paper for warmth. There was no basement under the back of the house, so we couldn't tell much from the inside either (at least, not without crawling through a two-foot-high "crawl space" under the floor, which I did not want to do in late fall). In our simplicity we believed ourselves equal to the task of repair. "We'll jack the house up," we told ourselves blithely. "The worst that can happen is that the house will fall down." This was a comfort, as we never believed it could happen. We were foolish children, I suppose. We were also right, although I find it harder to believe now than I did then.

But you see, I remembered my father's control over the buildings he owned. When he and his brother needed new silos on their farm, they put them up themselves. When these grew too small, they hitched a cable around them and pulled them down with a tractor, and put up a bigger one. They bought it off another farmer, dismantled it, and rebuilt it on their farm. When my parents moved off the farm, they took an 8×12 foot chicken coop along.

During the early spring we discussed, rationally and at great length, all possible foreseeable problems. We didn't know it then, but most of these foreseeable problems just weren't problems, as you will see. The first *practical* thing we did, late in the spring, after the unusually heavy rains had stopped, was to pull the tar paper off the back of the house to see what was what. We found rot behind it; siding, support beams, sill, all rotted, gone entirely in places. I suppose the wall stayed up by hanging from the roof.

We were still confident, and began to get things ready. I talked with my father about building jacks (a heavy jack, similar to a car jack). Farmers always have a building jack or two around to level up a sagging shed, so with a few calls, my father turned up seven mechanical type building jacks of assorted sizes.

Meanwhile, we took siding off the house so we could start. I have no magic advice for removing clapboards. They are put on bottom one first, then the next one overlapping that, then the next, and so on to the top of the house. The only neat way to take them off is to reverse the procedure: take off the top one, then the next one down, and the next, and so on to the bottom. We started halfway down.

Then we took off the rough siding. This is just what you would guess, a siding of rough finished wood underneath the outside siding. In new houses it is usually plywood; in older ones "shiplap," single boards, which fit together.

We found that to keep warm, earlier occupants had stuffed rags and scraps of insulation into the holes left by the rot. These held water beautifully and speeded up the rotting process. We pulled out these (and mouse skulls). At last the true extent of the damage was visible.

I'll need a few technical terms here. The *sill* of the house is the lowest wooden part of the house; it is the part that actually sits on the foundation. The framework of the house, including the floor beams, all rest on it. In newer houses it is usually a 2×8 plank. In our house it was an 8×8 beam. *Studs* are the upright 2×4s in the walls of a house. They're nailed vertically on the sill, and the inside and outside walls are nailed to them.

Well, two feet of our sill was completely gone—rotted away, the whole 8×8 inch mass of it. More was weak. Studs in the wall were rotten on the bottoms. Where the floor beams should have connected with the missing sill, the ends were rotted off. One floor beam in particular, which supported both the kitchen sink and the bathtub, was held up at one end only. I would have said the floor itself held up the sink and tub, but under the sink the floor, too, had rotted away. I asked our plumber what held up our sink. "Imagination," he snorted. And the foundation itself was tipped away from the house.

"When do you want to start?" my father asked us.

"As soon as it's dry," we answered, and prayed for rain. But clear weather came. Early one sunny morning my father showed up, his car trunk loaded with jacks.

"I'm ready," he said. I took him to the back of the house. He looked at it. "That's a big job there," he said. I nodded. "That's a big job," he said once again, and we started. We cleared away some rubble that had once been foundation. This opened a hole into the crawl space and gave us some room under the sill to position jacks.

It *was* a big job, so my father had asked a friend, a carpenter, to stop in and give us some advice. Soon he came.

"That's a big job," he whistled. My father and I both nodded. "Your main problem's here," he said, pointing to where the sill had rotted away. "Put a jack on each side of the break, so you can bring both parts up together." He cleared a small space under a beam, made sure the ground was firm, put a heavy two-inch plank down and leveled it up with small rocks. When he was sure the plank was solid and about level, he put the jack on it, put another heavy plank on top (to keep the jack from denting the beam), screwed the jack up as far as he could with his hand, then put a wrecking bar (that's just a heavy iron bar) into the hole provided and started turning.

As we screwed up the jack (this was surprisingly easy),

the house creaked and groaned, and you could see the whole thing going up! Then we put another jack under the sill on the other side of the break, and jacked that up even with the first part. Now the weight of the sill was entirely on these jacks, the sill itself was about half an inch above the foundation, where it existed.

"If I were you, I'd try putting another jack here." Our friend pointed.

We did so. Actually, it was clear where to put it. You see, a house is just a box, a properly built house, anyway. The walls and floor and roof are rigid, within limits. Lift one corner of the bottom and you'll also lift the roof, and much of the side walls. A house generally just sits on its foundation; it isn't nailed down. It weighs enough to stay put. If a giant wanted to pick up a house and set it down again unharmed, he could. But the rot had destroyed the structure of our house; it was no longer a proper box.

If we jacked up one side of the broken sill, there was no guarantee the rest would come along. Consequently, we put the jacks under all the separate parts that had once joined but did so no longer, to bring them to the same level, so we could raise them all together. We positioned a few extra jacks in other places to take some of the weight off the jacks we were primarily interested in.

Then we worked each jack in turn so all parts of the house came up together. It's easy to tell when you've worked one jack enough and should go on to the next: it gets very hard to turn. The other jacks will by then be easy. Work one of these until it, too, gets hard to turn, then go on to the next, and so on. Of course, we had to make sure each jack was *on* something *solid* and was level. By the way, look at your jacks before you start, so you don't screw them up too far: they come apart. If you reach the upper limits of a jack, take some cement blocks and flat rocks and build a temporary support pillar next to the jack. Ease up on the jack and let the beam down onto the pillar. Take the jack out and put a cement block or some planks where it was, then put the jack on it and start jacking again.

We raised the house an inch or more. It was now well off its foundation. We took wrecking bars and sledge hammers and knocked a considerable stretch of foundation apart. I crawled under the floor and put a few more jacks in obvious places—under beams that had little support now that the sill had been raised, and at the corner of the house where we knew the floor was not level. Of course one does not jack up a house using a light beam. Look for beams that support others—those are the ones to work on.

Each house is different, and old houses can be weird. One of our neighbors jacked a room up but did not check the inside as he worked. He found the floor had been built separately from the walls, and had been left behind as the rest of the room rose. He should have put jacks under the main floor beams as well as under the walls. Study your house carefully. A little sense goes a long way; a little common sense goes even further!

My big worry, as the house rose, was water pipes, but ours were fairly flexible and bent as the house rose. We never broke one. I was concerned about heating ducts too, but this was needless. What is attached to the floor goes up with the floor. That includes heating ducts, much of the plumbing and wiring. The *real* problem was drains, since these were fastened to the floor *and* went into the ground. I decided not to do anything about them unless they broke. This was probably not wise, but, as it happened, they did not break.

By noon, the house was up about half a foot and looked nearly level from the outside. The sag in the roof was gone. The second floor looked almost level. We were satisfied, my father and I. From here on, any more would be fine tuning. I was hardly ready to believe it had taken only one morning, but there it stood, a level house. We were ready for lunch, when Greer stuck her head out of the kitchen window. "The cupboard doors are all stuck," she wailed. But the house looked great.

Beginning the Rebuilding

Well, the house was level, but our work had hardly begun. The rotten wood had to be removed, the box-like structure of the building restored, a new foundation built, and siding replaced. The dramatic part was done, now it was time for the drudgery.

As openers we had to eliminate every bit of rot. Rot spreads. First the sill. We decided where it was sound by sticking it with a screwdriver: if it went in up to the elbow it was very bad; if it went in a little it was a little bad; if it didn't go in at all, it was good. (Use this test when you buy a house too. And don't stick the blade in across the grain!) Then we sawed away the bad parts. We now had a ten-foot gap in the sill that we would eventually fill with sound wood.

Next we worked on the wall studs. These were bad for about half a foot at the bottom, so we sawed them off just above this point. Finally we did the same with the floor beams. Now the rot had been removed from the structural parts of the house.

Then we tackled the floor. We decided to let the bathroom wait another year, but the kitchen floor couldn't wait, it had holes in it. So, early one day our plumber stopped by and disconnected the kitchen sink for us, leaving the bathroom plumbing usable. (Since then I've learned more about plumbing, and I think I could now do this myself.) We picked up the horribly rusted sink, carried it out to the trunk of my father's car, and happily drove the vile thing to the dump.

I cut away the bad flooring around the sink, I cut a

one-inch-thick piece of plywood to fit into the hole and rested it on floor beams.

We happened to have another sink on hand, one that had sat on the front porch. We painted it, and our plumber installed it. Our kitchen was usable again. The sink worked. The floor was sound. Linoleum will one day cover the plywood. We had been without a sink a day and a half.

Getting Our Footing

Now that the kitchen sink was in and life could go on with some sense of normalcy, it was time to build a new foundation. My father and I estimated how many concrete blocks we would need. (We didn't use them all, but you'll find them handy to have around. You can use them to build shelves in a hurry, or to tie the new puppy to. All kinds of things.) And we ordered concrete.

One morning, the supplies came, my father showed up, and we began. A foundation should go below the frost line, the depth to which the ground freezes in winter. Otherwise the foundation might shift around a bit. If you're starting fresh, you should dig a trench and start your foundation in it: four feet is a reasonable depth in our area, I'm told. Ask around to find out what the local practice is. We were lucky, the underground part of our old foundation was still good, so we could leave it alone and build on top.

A foundation begins with a footing. This is basically a flat bed of concrete that the concrete blocks sit on. The whole weight of the house ultimately rests on this footing; it distributes the weight over the ground below it. I'll tell you first how a footing is supposed to be laid, then I'll tell you what we did.

You start by building "forms," into which wet concrete can be dumped. These are composed of sides of scrap boards, held in place by stakes driven into the ground. They have no bottoms. The tops of the forms are made level, and at the height the footing is supposed to be. Then they are filled to the brim with concrete (mixed with stray rocks, to save money); it is smoothed off, it sets, the forms are pulled off and you have your footing.

This naturally leads me to a discussion of concrete. Cement is what a cement plant produces. If it is mixed with water a chemical reaction takes place and it hardens. In practice, cement alone is too expensive, so it is mixed with sand, gravel, or crushed stone, rocks, or boulders, depending on whether you are building a sidewalk or a power dam. The Romans sometimes used broken statues, which delights archeologists. Thus, in practice, the cement is what "cements" this other stuff together.

Concrete is simply a cement-sand or cement-gravel or cement-sand-gravel mixture. Typical proportions for most work are 1:2:3, that is, one part cement, two parts sand, and three parts gravel, by volume. But other proportions are often used, 1:3:6 for example is good for footings. The purpose of a cement mixer is to mix the cement with this other stuff, and eventually with water. But you can buy bags of cement-sand mix (as well as other combinations), and then you just add water, which is easy. Or you can buy cement itself and mix in gravel or crushed stone yourself, without a cement mixer, by dumping it all in a wheelbarrow and stirring it with a hoe. Or, if you need larger quantities you can buy up to whole truckloads of whatever mixture you decide you'll need from companies that sell pre-mixed concrete.

The people who sold us the concrete blocks told us how much to buy. For the footing, we decided a concrete-crushed stone mixture was good. We mixed these together, dry, in a wheelbarrow, using a hoe. Then we added water. This is done by making a hole in the middle of the mixture, squirting in some water, stirring this around, making another hole, adding more water, stirring this, and so on until enough water has been added. If you add lots of water at once it will be hard to mix. If you find you have added too much water, add more cement—that's fair. The final product should be somewhat thicker than soft ice cream. It should *not* be runny.

We hosed off the rocks on which the footing was to go, then we shoveled our concrete mixture into our forms. We used up a couple of bags of cement. After we smoothed off the top of our filled-up forms we were done for a day or two. We hosed off our tools immediately. Then we had lunch.

By the way, the "setting" of concrete is not a drying process; it is a chemical reaction and will go on even in the rain. In fact, during this reaction, concrete shouldn't dry out, or the reaction will stop. So, for a few days, while the concrete "cures," it should be left covered with damp feed bags or old blankets. Watertight plastic will also serve. This "curing" can be considered finished after seven days. We used an old plastic tablecloth.

Building the Foundation Wall

The following morning we figured the footing was ready to build on. Although the concrete had to "cure" for seven days, our footing would not bear much weight for several days, even if we started the wall, so we figured it was okay. We began work and had reached the third row of concrete block when Greer came by. "How's it look?" I asked.

"Well, I don't know," she replied. "It . . . ah . . . goes uphill, doesn't it?"

"Won't hurt anything," I snorted. "And anyway, it doesn't." But I knew it did. And so did my father. We'd been trying to pretend we didn't.

"At least it's in back of the house," Greer said sadly.

"I guess we better start over," I said. "Even if this worked, I wouldn't want to show it to anybody."

"Good," my father said. So we took the wall apart. We just picked the blocks off, hosed the still wet concrete away, and we were back where we started.

Our footing was not level; we had been careless with the forms, but it could be corrected. We slapped concrete on top of our unlevel footing. The slope was not enough, we thought, to build new forms. We did it freehand. For a final measure we laid a board on top of the wet concrete and put the level on it. It seemed okay. We took the board off and quit for the day.

"It never would have looked right," my father said. We all agreed.

Building the Foundation Wall Again

A few days later we started again. The procedure was much as before, but now our footing was level and things went well. We laid a bed of fresh concrete, about half an inch deep, on our *level* footing. Then we pressed a concrete block in this (wetting the block first) and tapped it level with the wooden handle of a trowel. Then we laid another block next to this, and soon the length of the footing was filled.

We had to put concrete between the blocks too. The way we did this was to stand a block on end, stick some concrete on the upright end of it, and hope it would stay put as we gently laid it in place on the footing. I eventually got so that I could manage this with a trowel most of the time, though my father persisted in using his fingers. And, by the way, concrete blocks are largely hollow. This makes them easier to handle, and, more important, actually makes a sort of insulation in a finished wall. Concrete alone lets cold through, but air space doesn't do this as well. The blocks are concave on the ends so that when two are butted together one more air pocket is created. These hollows are not filled up with anything; they are left empty.

"Wish we could have watched a real mason lay a wall first," my father said. "They just sort of zip, slap, bang—and it's right."

"Um," I grunted, and went zip, slap, splash with the trowel, swore, and scraped up the mess.

Well, one way and another, the lowest course of block got laid. We put a long board on this to see if it was even, and a level on top of the board. We had learned our lesson. It was okay, so we started on the next row up. We spread wet concrete on the blocks we had just laid, using trowel and finger. We did not fill up the air spaces, or hollows, of the blocks with concrete, though sometimes some dropped in.

"A real professional would just leave it there," my father said, carefully retrieving some concrete he had dropped inside a block.

Well, we laid the second row of block. Once in a while we needed to cut a block in order to end a row properly. The technique for this is simple. Take a hammer and a cold chisel and score the block lightly all the way around where you want the cut to be. Then go over this again and make your line deeper. Then again, and again. Fairly soon, your block will just fall in two neatly. Don't try to cut too deeply all at once.

In this fashion three rows of blocks went up and our new foundation was in place. We used the leftover wet concrete to patch cracks in the older parts of the foundation all around the house. Then we hosed off our tools and just stood there and looked at our work. Our new foundation was good. It was level. It was sound. It was solid. But best of all, it was beautiful.

The Letdown

With the new foundation in place, the rest was easy. I made a new sill, using a 2 × 6 plank, laying it along the new stretch of foundation, the bottoms of the new and old sills being at the same level.

With a new sill in place, I now repaired the wall studs whose bottoms I'd sawed off. For each one I cut a short length of 2 × 4 which would fill the gap between it and the sill lightly. Then I cut longer lengths of 2 × 4 and nailed them to each side of the joint thus made (this is called "splicing"). I also nailed the new lower part of the stud to the new sill. In this way each stud was spliced to its proper full length.

Now all the structural work was done. The house was again a box. I called to Greer, "I'm going to take the jacks out. Want to watch?"

She ran out holding the baby and stood there waiting. One by one I screwed the jacks down and took them out. It took a couple of minutes. "Okay, I'm done."

"You mean that's all?" she asked.

"That's all," I answered. It was certainly a most undramatic symbolic act. Still, one must make the best of the few ceremonies permitted us in these unromantic days. We kissed and had lunch.

What remained to be done was sealing the house wall against the weather. We began by stapling roll insulation into all the open parts of the wall we could get at.

Next I nailed up rough siding. I used shiplap, similar to that which came off the house. This siding came down to the sill and closed up the wall opening. Over the shiplap we stapled waterproof paper.

I bought new clapboards to match the siding on that part of the house and nailed them up. I reversed proper procedure and put in the top board first because I was trying to line these up with siding already in place. I nailed them loosely so I could wiggle them if necessary to get the boards lower down up into place. When all were in place, I nailed them down tightly. This outermost siding came down far enough to cover the sill and keep it dry.

A few observations. If the positioning of one clapboard is off, you will also be off in all the rest; indeed, the error tends to get worse as you go on. Also, even though the width of the new clapboards was right, they did not exactly match the old ones—their contours were somewhat different. They were close enough so that one is not likely to notice, however. If you want perfection you may have to get the things milled specially.

Next I puttied the cracks between the ends of the new clapboards and the ends of the old. After a few days, I gave all the new wood a coat of primer paint. Later in the summer we gave the entire house a badly needed paint job so that the scars of our surgery are no longer visible. The house now not only *is* healthy, it looks healthy too.

The beginning of this project, jacking up the house, had been spectacular. The end came with a whisper. I washed out my paint brush, looked at what we had done, and realized there was no more to do.

The next day my parents stopped by. They'd been busy at their house for a few days and hadn't been able to help us. My father looked at the back of the house. "Why, it's all done," he said. He sounded disappointed.

I nodded and sat down to admire our work.

"Oh, come on now," my father said. "You can't be tired. You're young yet." (My father is seventy-five.)

I began to get suspicious.

"Have you got the paint for the roof yet? I've got some brushes in the car." He looked up at the roof. "Gonna be a big job," he announced.

CHAPTER 2

GROOMING THE LAND TO FIT OUR NEEDS

Greer speaking

Among the things we really needed, coming as we did from a very crowded city, was a sense of space. This was part of mental health for us. At first we found that our need of a sense of space was filled adequately by the *idea* of owning fifty-four acres of land. Mel would point to some tree off in the distance and say, "That's *our* tree. Do you realize what that means? It's *our* tree." But that was very early in the game.

We—and especially I, who had grown up in the city—found it necessary to be able to *get to* that particular tree. Images are not necessarily reality, I realized, coming from a family of artists.

In any case, when Mel and I moved to the country, I needed to feel that tree, smell it, bump into it, examine it closely to believe it was really what it seemed to be. That tree, off in the distance, was presumably alive. I wasn't willing to take it on faith. I had to go up close and see for myself that it was alive and what it seemed to be.

But to get to that tree off in the distance, even if on paper it was ours, was not as simple as it might seem. There were enormous obstacles in the way of getting there. We were extraordinarily house-centered. The laundry had to get done. The house had to be made livable and safe and comfortable. These were needs, too. And since they were close at hand, right under our noses, it was easy to get actually *stuck* in the house. The need to get out and examine that particular tree was felt strongly enough to create conflict, but not strongly enough to overcome the almost fatal magnetism of the house.

There were other difficulties as well. There are different kinds of stamina. While I am capable of sitting for ten or twelve hours typing, I found that a fraction of that time beating my way through dense brush and bumpy-floored forestlands was exhausting, even if it was exhilarating. Outdoor living requires a different style of breathing. Walking in field and forest is genuinely different from walking on concrete. I had to learn to balance differently; I had to watch for different things: giant ant hills, hidden branches, bogs, animal holes, even abandoned open well pits from houses which have disappeared. While developing these different reflexes and habit patterns, I found that tremendous physical and emotional energy was called into play, even after we'd managed to break loose from the house's magnetism for an hour or so.

Of course, I wouldn't have described it this way at first. It never occurred to me to describe it at all, except in certain ill-natured squawks to the effect that, "If I don't get out this minute, I'll scream!" after fussing away half the day, then, once out, equally ill-natured squawks after the fifth time I'd stumbled over something or other during what I'd previously envisioned as a "relaxing" stroll on our land.

Nature has very little patience for this kind of problem. Every inch of the land was bristling with life. I didn't know where to put my feet. It wasn't that I was timid about stepping on living things, it was just that the brush was so thick, fallen branches and jutting rocks were disguised so well by the thick covering of leaves that I couldn't manage my body anymore. I had to fight my way through, and they'd trip me up. There didn't seem to be *room* for me. All the room was taken up by the profusion of things totally different from me. In short, in trying to get to that tree we supposedly owned, in trying to grab on physically to that sense of space we had acquired, I, at least, was getting the opposite message. There really *wasn't* space for me. I could beat my way through, certainly, and be a spectator from the outside, but I had no place there, really, except as a somewhat masochistic voyeur.

Which is what I was, at that point. But those early, frustrating walks were necessary. Both Mel and I learned a lot from them. We were beginning to understand a few things, and that understanding was beginning to unsnarl a few of the tangles in our heads.

Getting a Perspective on the Land

Although the exultation of "reaching that tree" was, for a time, unobtainable, we were slowly but surely, almost in spite of ourselves, gaining that sense of space. We were getting a feeling for the land on those walks—the land in its own moods, the land exhibiting its own specialties and talents without interference. What we were seeing was the rhythm of reforestation.

Our land had been farmland, but it had been very marginal farmland indeed. Mountaintops are not known for good, thick topsoil and they *are* known for rocks. Some of our land probably always had been wooded. Other parts had been "let go" at different times, so every stage in between was evident.

For instance, in back of the house stretched a marshy area, which in spring is a small stream. Then came a belt of what had obviously been pasture areas, all carefully marked off by stone walls and fallen barbed wire fencing. These walls were now within the tree line, since the woods surrounding the pasture areas had spread, and a ring of young trees was slowly tightening around the clear areas, choking out the blackberry and raspberry bushes which love to grow around the edges of clear fields. Even in the centers of those fields there were shoulder-high trees scattered around. But predominant in those fields was the brush: woody-stemmed bushes, mostly blueberries and something which my neighbors call "hard hack." It was obvious which fields had been "let go" first. The trees were higher, thicker, and the brush and berry bushes were being choked out. Walking was more difficult.

Beyond the belt of former pasture lay woodlot. Even here we found the character differed from area to area. There were some areas which were still bushy, but were also very dense with tall but skinny (and therefore young) trees. Then we'd stumble over a crumbled stone wall and find bigger trees, and very little undergrowth.

Slowly we began to accept the fact that if we wanted room on our land we would have to work ourselves and our needs into the scheme of things. We began to see how to do this. And as the vision formed, we found we had achieved our long-sought sense of space without knowing it. The way we discovered it was that we got lost—and had to find our way home again. ("We live on *top* of the mountain, so if we keep going *up* we're bound to get home," said Mel. "Do you remember where the sun was with respect to the house when we left?" I asked. "No, of course not," Mel said. I didn't either. After three hours of wandering, we found our way out, and when we did, Mel exclaimed happily, "Imagine! Getting lost in your own backyard!" We bragged about it to our city friends for weeks thereafter. We were getting our country legs.

Developing an Aesthetic

As we gained perspective on our land, we began to develop a country aesthetic. It was this aesthetic which let us see how we could adjust ourselves to our land, and adjust the land to fill at least some of our needs. This sounds a little academic, but I firmly believe it is God's truth.

There is one aesthetic which goes something like this: "This is man's world. He should profit by it. The productions of man are good and are beautiful. Man should print his image all over the place, and especially on nature. And he should grow Christmas trees." And this aesthetic does lead to acres of Christmas trees planted in neat rows, periodically thinned and groomed for a good investment.

But we suspected that this kind of aesthetic also led to certain kinds of reactions, and it was those we instinctively feared. It isn't our way. We wanted space, but we didn't want *that* kind of space. Just enough to be able to enjoy our land, to have a small share in its resources, and to be able to share in its secrets a little. So the aesthetic we arrived at was more like this: "This is nature's world. The productions of nature are good. Nature *will* dominate this world whether man likes it or not, so it is up to man to fit into nature, since, after all, he is of nature." And this aesthetic led us to certain kinds of plans. Since these plans formed gradually, we weren't completely overwhelmed by them into non-action, as we had been at first. We just began doing things here and there, seeing how it went, and changing our techniques as we went along. We found out that the first time we tried something it seemed impossible. But always after a while, we'd learn how, and what had been impossible became matter of course. Our plans are still shifting around and maturing, but to give an idea of where we're going I'll spin some of them for you.

The Fruits of the Field

What did we want? We wanted food, warmth, recreation. This meant firewood, berries and other wild foods, an orchard, gardens, pastures, pleasant walks and a lawn area. It became obvious that many of these could be combined. For instance, there is a path leading from the back of our house over the spring stream and marshy area, out into a field ringed by young trees.

The path goes along the edge of this field, and out to a dirt road which is one of the boundaries of our property. Since we wanted to keep this path open, and didn't own a gas powered sicklebar mower, Mel had to learn to use a grass scythe. He bought one and spent an afternoon messing around with it, and got pretty good at it (sharpen it frequently and swing with the blade parallel to the ground). He now mows that path once or twice a year so it doesn't grow up to brush. So far so good.

The field has plenty of high-bush blueberries, not to mention strawberries, low-bush blueberries, and a crawling kind of blackberry. The brush and small trees make it hard to pick the berries, so we decided to make footpaths from blueberry bush to blueberry bush, and to clear around the bushes themselves. This means going out with nippers and a pruning saw and cutting out the small trees and bushes, then keeping them cut every year. It is a slow process, but eventually we will have that field honeycombed with grassy footpaths which will make harvesting easy, and as a bonus will provide easy paths for cross-country skiing in winter. The small trees will make good firewood for the cookstove. We will fence part of the field and fatten a steer there.

Additional firewood from this field will come from the overflow from the woodlot that rings the field. Once the trees are cut back to the stone wall, the blackberry and raspberry bushes that are languishing can revive and give us more fruit. I might even set out a few more varieties when we get the edge cleared.

We set out two trees in the field this past spring: a mulberry tree and a walnut tree, and next year I'll set out two or three more. The following year, we'll order an orchardful, making sure to include a few trees for bird food . . . so we don't have to fight over the crop.

One of the reasons we decided on the minimal change method of doing things rather than the more traditional clear-everything-out-and-set-out-the-orchard technique was our experience camping a few years ago. We camped in an abandoned orchard. Other trees had grown up in and amongst the apple trees. Those apples were not wormy, though they were never sprayed. I suspect it was the variety of different trees around that protected the apple trees. For the same reason I'll never remove *all* the hard hack bushes from the blueberry field. Our blueberries are not wormy, and the hard hack just might have something to do with that fact.

It would have been a real mistake for us to start on any of this the first year. That full year of poking around and watching was necessary. We didn't know enough about plants. We didn't want to get into the situation of cutting down all the elderberry bushes because they weren't blueberries, if you get my meaning.

So much for my sense of space. I'll talk about my other involvements with the land later.

CHAPTER 3

HOW
WE KEEP
CHICKENS

Greer speaking

When we finally decided to try keeping chickens, whole new vistas opened up. It was a milestone in our homesteading careers. Properly managed, keeping chickens is as easy as keeping a dog, maybe easier.

Mel knew nothing about chickens, except that they are stupid birds. Mel's father had kept hundreds of chickens back on the farm, but Mel had been too young to remember. My only experience with chickens was a single visit to a chicken farm when I also was very young. I remember being chased by a chicken whose head had been cut off. But trauma, after all, fades, so we consulted Mel's father and some books.

We found out that after chickens have been laying one

23

year, their egg production tapers off, but they still eat just as much. So it is more economical for big chicken farms to sell off these "used" chickens than to keep them going. We bought thirty of these chickens from a local chicken farm. We figured we would slaughter the worst and keep the best for laying hens. We paid 50¢ each, but the price has gone up to 75¢ recently; two years ago, it was a quarter.

There are many kinds of chickens, we discovered. Good sources of information are Sears' and Ward's special *farm* catalogs. Some varieties are better for eggs, some are better for meat. Ours are white leghorns, which make good egg layers, but they are not the best for meat; there's not much on them. If you buy "used" hens, it is almost certain you'll get an egg-type chicken. While I'm on this topic, you should also know some kinds of chickens lay white eggs, some brown, and some speckled. It doesn't make any difference to the inside of the egg.

We brought our hens home live in crates (supplied by us). We didn't need a rooster, since we didn't need fertile eggs to raise chicks from.

Chickens, like everyone else, have certain needs. I wasn't surprised when Mel's father informed me that unhappy chickens don't lay well. I had, after all, breast-fed a baby. So the first thing we needed to know was what makes a chicken happy. Then maybe we would get eggs.

Well, chickens need a coop. We housed the flock in a second-hand portable coop. It was too small, it turned out, and had other major drawbacks. It took us a full month to learn what makes chickens happy. During that month we learned a number of unpleasant facts of life.

I'd been informed in very graphic terms that chickens are canabalistic. They've been known to peck each other to death. It turned out that our used chickens had been "debeaked." No, this doesn't mean that their beaks had been removed, merely that they had been trimmed—sort of rounded off—so they couldn't draw blood when they pecked. They definitely are not friendly with each other.

Another disturbing fact of life is that unhappy chickens not only don't lay well, but when they do manage to squeeze out an egg they often eat it.

A particularly unpleasant fact of life is that chickens are dirty. They foul their own nests, food, water, and everything else handy quite cheerfully. If the henhouse is not convenient to clean (and ours wasn't by any means), life becomes very sad, especially on hot, moist days.

Finally Mel solved our collective problems. He designed and built a truly wonderful henhouse. It is an italic A-frame (that is, its ridge pole is off-center, so the block of four nests can be off to one side). It is roofed with red asphalt roofing paper, has chicken-wire ends (for ventilation—very important in chicken houses) and a chicken-wire floor (to make cleaning easier). It has a large door for us to gather eggs from on one side, and a small door leading to a chicken-wire–fenced yard on one side. The house has roosts (long poles for the chickens to perch on) at various heights well away from the food. He planned better than four square feet per hen, and the house stands five feet high.

The henhouse was a summer success. In a day or two after we moved them into their new quarters the chickens settled down. Egg production went up, and soon we were supplying Mel's parents, too. The birds gained weight. They looked healthy, and, if possible, happy. Caring for them in their new home was simple, even pleasant.

Chicken droppings are traditionally an unpleasant problem. They accumulate quickly and sometimes produce a strong ammonia smell. Our henhouse has a chicken-wire floor so droppings fall through and the birds don't walk in them. The house itself is up on concrete blocks, so there is plenty of room underneath for droppings, and fresh air can get at them. No ammonia smell gets started. Once every two or three months we rake out underneath the buildings and cart the droppings to the compost pile, where, after proper aging, they become excellent garden fertilizer.

Chickens need access to fresh water. We found it was not sufficient just to put out a dish of water. They'd perch on the edge and knock it over. A small pail did the job for a while, but it meant changing the water several times a day, as they perched on the edge and dirtied it. Finally we ended up buying a chicken waterer, a device that automatically feeds fresh water as the exposed water is drunk up. It costs about six dollars and doesn't require electricity or batteries. It made life a lot simpler.

We had to buy chicken feed (we store it in garbage cans). We had been given a chicken feeder. Ours is a long, narrow trough with a pole over it so the chickens can get their heads in to eat, but not their feet. Chickens instinctively scratch for their food. They're built that way. If we just put a pan of food out they'd stand in it and scratch around and dirty it up, not to mention dumping it out. We kept the chicken trough filled with a ground chicken feed blended especially for laying hens, called laying mash. We also learned to give them a pan of this laying mash moistened until it was lumpy, into which we mixed table scraps chopped fine, including the last drops from milk cartons, chopped bits of meat and fat, and vegetable peelings. (Chickens will eat a wide variety of things. Don't give them coarse things, like onion or tomato peels, or stuff like tea leaves or coffee grounds; anything else seems to go, though.) In addition to the wet mash and dry mash, we also give them "scratch" feed, scattered on the ground of their yard. When feed companies stopped making prepared scratch feed mix, because of the wheat shortage, we switched to cracked corn for scratch. They like it well enough, but one veteran chicken raiser tells us it is too fattening to be ideal chicken food.

The chickens relish green food, too. We give them turnip tops, carrot tops, radish tops and tender grass in season. It got so all I had to do was say "radish" and the chickens would come piling out of their house for their greens ration.

Since birds eat grain and don't have teeth, they require fine pebbles to help them grind up their food. They eat these pebbles. Also, when a chicken is laying a lot of eggs, she needs calcium from which to construct egg shells. If she doesn't get the calcium she will lay very thin-shelled eggs for a time, and finally will begin laying Dali-esque soft eggs. We combined these two needs and supplied the hens with broken up oyster shells. A friend who no longer keeps chickens gave us a bucketful of these, and a self-feeding hopper. It requires filling once every few weeks.

I developed a solution to the egg-eating problem. If an egg showed signs of being pecked at, we'd check the oyster shell dispenser to make sure it was full, and we'd mix some meat (frequently canned dog food) into their wet mash the next day. This is almost always enough to stop the egg pecking. We've heard there are sometimes problems with chronic egg eaters, hens who develop a real preference for eggs. None of ours have. We did run across a suggested remedy in an old book, but we've never had occasion to try it. Here it is, though, just in case. Break the egg carefully and remove the contents. Beat this up with powdered mustard, then refill the eggshell with the mixture, seal the break, and put the loaded egg back in a nest. It sounds like a mouthful ought to convince a hen not to repeat the experiment of egg eating, but, as I said, we haven't tried it.

The other solution we've heard, also a traditional one, is keep watch and find out who it is, then have her for supper. A good preventive to egg eating is make sure to gather the eggs several times daily. Hens are imitative creatures, and a flock tends to lay all its eggs in one or two nests. If the nest is too full an egg can accidentally break, the chickens will eat it, and off you go.

Late in the summer, we tried the experiment of letting the chickens roam the backyard. It worked well. Our feed bills dropped. The birds were living off the land in about the same proportions as we were. They didn't go near the garden, but preferred to roam in the lilac bushes. They liked the cover, I suppose. At sundown they'd go into their henhouse of their own accord. They also returned to the henhouse when they wanted to lay—at least we never found eggs in the lilac bushes. We did learn not to let them out if we were going away for the afternoon, however, once we experienced the difficulty of catching loose chickens. A flying tackle won't work, because a chicken is better at flying than we are at tackling. They half run, half fly at surprising speeds. You have to saunter after them casually, herding them where you want them to go.

Mel had designed the new henhouse for summer use only. We planned to slaughter the birds in the fall and buy new ones in the spring. About this time we were sparring gingerly with the idea of getting a goat. We began to think about building a combination goat shed and winter chicken coop—some day.

The price of eggs shot up that summer. We did some calculations and discovered we actually were saving money by having chickens, even though we had to buy chicken feed (which is not chicken feed, so to speak). We weren't saving much, but it was something. And fresh eggs really taste better. We decided to winterize the henhouse and keep the birds.

In the fall we stapled scrap plastic over both ends of the henhouse. Later, when cold weather hit, we sealed about the base with boards. Mel ran electricity out there, so in very cold weather we can burn a heat lamp or two. A heat lamp pointed at their food and water keeps it from freezing. It doesn't take much. Hens generate a lot of heat, and the plastic keeps most of it from escaping.

The hens went through a month of moulting in late fall, so egg production dropped for a while, but they started laying again at Christmas. Normally we can count on between six and eight eggs a day from our fourteen "used" hens.

Caring for the chickens in their new quarters is easy. Once a day we feed the birds—scratch feed in the yard, laying mash and left-overs in a pan, greens in season. We see they have clean water and oyster shells. Because of the wire floor that Mel installed, we rake out the droppings only every month or two (depending on the weather). The routine: feed the chickens late in the morning, gather eggs throughout the day at random. It is simple and satisfying.

Hen in the Course of Human Events

We bought thirty chickens. Fourteen are laying for us. The rest have been internalized. Here's how we did it.

In a way, the whole experience of slaughtering chickens was a test for us. We have long been irritated by people who sit down to a nice meal of steak or fried chicken and discuss how cruel it is to slaughter animals for meat. We are, after all, carnivores. We've met people who are franker about their double standard: they will cheerfully eat meat, but will not from any animal they have "met." I have much more respect for a friend of Mel's, a cheerful carnivore, who told me of an incident with his father. A squirrel had been raiding the bird feeder. The friend's father got out his air gun. He didn't mean to kill the squirrel, merely to frighten it away.

But he charged up the air gun too much and shot the squirrel dead. "He felt awfully bad about killing that squirrel. He went and got it, cleaned and skinned it and cooked it up and ate it. My father really impressed that on me as a child—if you kill something you eat it, and it's the only reason you kill, that's that." Mel's friend learned that lesson well, and knows a lot about what it means to be alive as a result. (He still provides some of the meat eaten in his household by hunting.) Face to face with two crates of chickens, we were to find out.

At issue, of course, was our ideal of self-sufficiency. If we couldn't manage to eat something we'd met, so to speak, there was no hope of growing our own meat. We could, of course, hire the slaughtering done, but that didn't really solve anything at all. We didn't want to get in the position of one family we know of who spent a lot of time and energy raising a pig. As is likely to happen with beginners, they made quite a pet out of that very intelligent animal. But they also spent enormous quantities of money feeding it special food so as to have really superb meat. When slaughtering time came they managed to swallow their consciences and took piggy to the butcher—he was getting *awfully* big. The lady of the house duly wrapped up her friend in freezer paper, stuck all his parts in the freezer. And there it stayed, yards of pork chops, hams, sausages, roasts and bacon. They could not bring themselves to eat it.

Finally, six months later, the man of the house got disgusted and insisted that they cook up some pork chops. The meat was so superb that the rest of the pig was eaten up in no time at all. The gourmet instinct had finally overcome the family's objections, and the pig did not die in vain after all. The moral of the story, of course, is: (1) don't make pets out of livestock intended to supply meat to the table; and (2) take good care to produce an extremely tasty product first time around—it helps a lot. But back to us and our chickens.

Slaughtering is not a neat affair. It is the least bucolic of our homesteading experience.

Mel does the slaughtering, and I'm in charge of plucking and drawing. Actually, Mel's parents came by to help us out, and we shared the meat. Mel, or his father, whosever turn it is, grabs a chicken, maneuvers it around until he has both feet and wing tips in his left hand. They say it is important to hold the wing tips because otherwise they flap and the chicken flops around. They lay it breast down on an old stump and cut off its head with a *sharp* hatchet. Mel says, "Then I sort of hurl the chicken down and throw a milk crate over it. I hold the crate down with my foot. The purpose of the crate is to keep the thing from running around." Mel carries the chicken around to the front yard and turns it over to Mel's mother and me.

Drawing a chicken is a smelly operation, so it is best done outdoors. We have a pail of hot water ready (the best temperature is about 140°; hotter might break the skin, cooler won't do the job). I hold the chicken by its feet and dip it into the hot water to loosen the feathers. (We know it has been in long enough by pulling some of the big wing feathers. If they come out easily, the chicken is ready. If they don't, it needs more time. If the feathers don't come out easily within a minute in the water, the water isn't hot enough. If this happens, get some hotter water and dunk the chicken again.)

Then Mel's mother and I scrape off the feathers (with the grain), and pull out any "pin" feathers that haven't come off. This last is a little tedious, and a beginner is apt to miss a number of these "pin" feathers, but practice makes perfect. What's left is beginning to resemble the whole chickens you see in the supermarket, with a few exceptions. First of all, there are tiny hairs sticking out of the skin, which Mel burns off with his propane torch, trying not to burn the skin in the process.

After that we gut the chickens. With a *sharp* knife, we

cut around the anus (which by this time looks startlingly familiar), being sure not to cut the intestines. Then we reach into the abdominal cavity and scoop out everything scoopable, gently, so as not to break the gall bladder, which contains the bile (if this is broken and gets on the meat it makes it bitter. If it does break, wash the gook off the chicken *immediately* with cold water). The gall bladder is a dark yellowish-green color. We detach the liver, giblet and the heart (squeeze out any clotted blood from the heart) from the mess, rinse them and put them in separate bowls. Sometimes we find eggs in various degrees of formation. Some actually have shells. Some are complete eggs, but instead of the shell they are surrounded by a soft membrane. Some are just yokes. All of these are eminently edible, so we have a bowl set up for them.

We also set up a container for chicken fat. We slit the membrane on the round giblet, peel out the little bag of gritty stuff inside (that gets thrown away), wash the giblet and put it in its bowl. We draw back the skin of the neck and remove the crop (a bag of undigested food) and pull out the windpipe. We cut the neck off short, and the most unpleasant part of the operation is now over. (Before the windpipe is removed, if we happen to hit the chest just right, a startlingly lifelike "squawk" emerges from the carcass.) We wash the chicken inside and out with a garden hose. When you get the hang of it, the whole process takes about twenty minutes. The first time, however, it is apt to take longer. Turkeys are drawn the same way, by the by. We bought our Thanksgiving turkey from a neighbor who raised a flock this year. What a difference in taste from those processed supermarket turkeys! It was heavenly. But back to the chickens.

We cut up the chickens with an eye to how we will use them. We set aside the necks, feet (don't throw them away, save them for soup), wings and backs plus any bones we remove from other parts. We will cook these down into soup stock when the rest of the chickens are packed safely away in the freezer. But meanwhile we wrap the breasts separately, some with bones, some without, for things like chicken curry and chicken kebob.

Then we clean up the mess, Mel's parents go home and I start the soup stock. I dip the chicken feet in boiling water for a few seconds and peel off the top layer of skin (it comes off very easily after scalding). I either cut off the toenails or I pull the top layer away with pliers, and stick the cleaned feet in my canner with all the bones, necks, backs, and wing tips I've set aside. I add water to cover and cook them at fifteen pounds pressure for about forty-five minutes.

I let the pressure go down of its own accord, then strain the soup. The stock I put in the refrigerator so the fat comes to the top and hardens a bit (chicken fat never gets very hard). Meanwhile I pick all the bones out of the meat, put the meat in freezer containers for chicken salad and creamed chicken and things like that. Then I skim the fat from the stock, heat the stock so it melts (the cool concentrate forms a jelly), and either can it or pour it into ice cube trays and freeze it. When it is frozen, I remove the cubes from the trays and put them in a plastic bag, tie it shut, label and date it, and put it in the freezer. Whenever I want a cup of soup I take out a couple of soup cubes, heat them with a cup of water and perhaps some dried minced vegetables (see chapter on drying), and salt it to taste. This is very good soup indeed! The soup cubes can also be used for gravies or whenever soup stock is called for.

CHAPTER 4

THE GARDENING PASSION

Greer speaking

It turns out that I am a born gardener. I can say this now, after two highly successful vegetable gardens. But in Yonkers, while we were waiting to move to the country, I had severe doubts about my gardening competence. I had never succeeded even in keeping a house plant alive.

"Don't worry," Mel said to me, "knowing you, if you can eat it you'll be able to grow it." Where I am concerned, Mel is frequently a true prophet.

I was still suspicious of the whole thing. "Well, I'm going to send for a book on gardening," I said.

"Send for a book," Mel replied.

I sent for a book. The book I sent for was the perfect book for me: Sam Ogden's *Step By Step to Growing Organic Vegetables* is ideal for a beginner. Another delightfully use-

35

ful book I turned up is Chico's *Organic Gardening and Natural Living,* by Frank (Chico) Bucaro and David Wallenchinsky. Ogden gardens in Vermont, and Chico gardens in California. These books contain somewhat different types of information—and between the two of them I, a rank amateur, managed to get a feeling for the gardening process. I recommend them highly! (See bibliography for details.) The valuable thing about the two books is that they tell about plants and dirt and insects and people and the relationship between all these things. Both authors are convinced that gardening is a simple and natural occupation which requires mostly good will sprinkled heavily with common sense—not to mention compost. They were *almost* enough to start me off. Mel's father did the rest by showing me some of the more obvious tricks of the trade that somehow never find their way into books. I'll get to these later.

As to being a born gardener, I don't know if that green thumb of mine would have showed up, say, ten years ago. Ten years ago, I had different goals, and somewhat different values. I also had less patience. And half or more of the gardening knack consists of patience.

I don't mean endurance. I don't even mean a willingness to do drudgery. I really mean patience. I suspect that endurance and a willingness to do drudgery might possibly substitute in part for this thing I call patience, at least in someone who had been bred to the art; but I doubt that they are adequate for a beginner.

Most of gardening involves waiting. You have to wait for the soil to get "ready" for tilling. You plant and wait for your seed to come up. Then you thin and weed the plants and wait until they are ready for use. Even then there is lots of waiting. You have to wait until the plants are dry before weeding or harvesting. Plants are vulnerable when wet. There is a hell of a lot of waiting involved. But there is another kind of patience—a patience *with yourself* which is necessary for a beginner to garden successfully! A neighbor came by once as Mel and I were sitting contemplating a newly planted garden and said (only half jokingly, I'm convinced), "It makes me mad the way you sit and look at your garden." She was in the process of wrestling with a "new" garden—that is, a garden which had been essentially wild pasture for years before. Later, out of my hearing, she explained further. With us sitting there sipping beer, looking on complacently as the plants began to grow, it seemed as if there were no *work* to gardening, somehow. That was the impression. She knew for a fact that it *was* work, and it should *seem* like work. The impression of leisure threw her off kilter.

Another new gardener complained to us one day that he wasn't cut out for "that sort of thing." "That sort of thing" consisted of getting things done. "Why, I must have wasted two hours today watching humming birds. Five minutes here, ten minutes there—it mounts up. And the garden is not getting in." But his garden *did* get in. He is "up-tight" because he doesn't yet realize that that five minutes here and ten minutes there watching will make him a much better gardener. It is an integral part of gardening. It is part of the patience involved in gardening.

Luckily I possess a large quantity of this particular sort of patience. At all stages of the garden's growth I sit and stare at it. And learn from it. This is almost as important as weeding, I find. It is during those periods of sitting and staring that I come to understand the plants and the whole garden as a successfully functioning organization: its crops, weeds, insects, birds. And I find it impossible to care adequately for anything or anyone I don't understand. It is, of course, a patience born of interest. Actually, sitting and staring at the garden is not very difficult—what *is* difficult about it is to accept it as a necessary and pleasurable part of gardening.

For us compulsives it is hard to get past the Puritan Ethic—
or is it the factory mentality?

I suspect that the most dangerous mistake a beginning
gardener will make is one of attitude. Before I came face to
face with the good earth, so to speak, I thought that people
had more to do with the plants they grow than they actually
do. I know this sounds funny, but I mean it. Terms like
"growing season" made absolutely no sense to me. My initial
idea was to "get the garden in early" and plant well into the
fall; anything else seemed like laziness and improvidence.

But there is such a thing as a growing season. I didn't
believe it until I saw it with my own eyes. It has to do with
the condition of the soil; obviously you can't till frozen soil.
But tilling muddy soil is worse than a waste of time; it packs
the earth down into something resembling a well-used dirt
road, and not much will grow on a road bed, that's for sure.
It has to do with the weather, of course. And it has to do with
the local insect and bird life cycles, and probably with half
a dozen other things I don't know about. But I *do* know that
seeds planted before the local growing season is in effect take
a long time to germinate (to start growing into plants); that
that they are usually less healthy than those planted during
more appropriate times. Also, I find that seeds planted at the
end of the growing season grow very sluggishly, and are not
as hardy or sturdy as those planted earlier. Of course, there
are mild differences in the growing seasons for different sorts
of plants; spinach and sweet peas hate hot weather, and
therefore have their "growing season" during spring or fall
cool weather. Tomatoes and beans can't stand frost, so can't
be put into the ground until the weather warms up. But on
the whole it is pretty uniform. Also, the growing season will
vary considerably according to locality. A friend down the
mountain (where it is slightly more temperate) has a magnificent garden. His garden is "ready" at least a month before
mine is, and he is less than ten miles away.

There is not only this business of the growing season. Plants, it turns out, have an enormous will to live. Given half a chance they will grab hold and fight dearly for life. They are not nearly as neurotic as people. But the idea of a garden is not only that the plant process enough food and light for its own survival, but that it process enough for us, too. So I arrange things so that the plants are given a good deal more than half a chance; I set things up so that the plants I am interested in have a particularly favorable environment. Then I let them thrive, which they are perfectly willing to do. My business as gardener, it turns out, is to get to understand what the various plants want and need, and to let them do their own thing, interfering only to maintain that favorable environment. I found I didn't have to "nurse" the garden along. After I had insured certain conditions, all that I did was to maintain them. I did very little interfering with the plants themselves.

I already had a philosophy of child rearing which seemed to work pretty well. Before Miriam was born, I decided on this course of action, and have found no cause to change it. I decided that I would do the *absolute minimum* necessary to keep her perfectly happy. For example, I wouldn't use oil or powder on her bottom unless she came down with diaper rash. The system worked so well that I decided to apply it to gardening. I would do the absolute minimum to keep the plants perfectly happy.

So I wouldn't play God. I wouldn't decide in advance that my plants needed certain chemicals and order them from a factory where they would be synthesized from petroleum. I wouldn't decide in advance birds were a problem and set up deterrents. I wouldn't decide in advance that bugs were a problem and spread around all sorts of poisons to kill them off before they showed up. And I wouldn't decide in advance that weeds were a problem and spray one sort of cancer-producing hormone in my corn field to kill off broad-leafed weeds, and another sort of cancer-producing hormone in my tomato bed to kill off narrow-leafed plants. I wouldn't even mulch (spread a thick layer of hay, black plastic, or leaves around the plants I wanted, to keep the weeds from getting the light to grow). I would work *with* the land, not in spite of it.

Nature is really very cooperative. For instance, she tries to supply soil lacks if left alone. For example, plants require nitrogen in the form of nitrate. If the nitrogen in the soil somehow becomes depleted, some plants will not thrive— and therefore not survive under competition—on that soil. But there are other plants (clover, the legumes—peas, beans, for instance) that team up with nitrogen-fixing bacteria to convert nitrogen from the air into nitrates, and store them in their roots. When these plants die and decay, the supply of nitrate then becomes available for other plants. So in a soil low in nitrogen, this "nitrogen fixing" sort of plant will have the advantage: it will grow vigorously, while others will not.

Some plants have shallow root systems. Others have deep root systems. If the surface of the soil somehow gets depleted, then the plants with shallow root systems will be at a disadvantage, and plants that "feed deep" will get their chance to take hold. As the seasons go by these will release stored food into the upper layers of the soil. And so it goes on.

Of course, when I gardened I would be interfering drastically with the process. Or would it be so drastic after all? I would plant a variety of plants in my garden, some nitrogen feeding plants, some nitrogen storing plants. Some would be surface feeding plants; some would be deep rooted, and therefore deep feeding. They would, true enough, be different plants from what would have grown there without my interference. But how much different? If the soil were not in appropriate condition for a certain type of plant, that plant would not grow well. And that would be a good clue that something else should be growing there. Indeed, if one plant does not grow well then other, more ecologically appropriate plants *will* grow there and *grow well*—and they would be weeds of various sorts. Those weeds are probably useful. But of course I could not let the weeds, for all their usefulness, crowd out my garden plants. Dilemma. How should I solve it?

I decided that this matter of weeding should be treated in the following manner. Before I planted the garden I would weed it very thoroughly, then plant my garden. At that point, then, the weeds and, the cultivated plants would be at equal advantage. Weed seeds that had not gotten a chance before the garden was tilled, and traces of roots, and seeds blown in by wind, weather and dropped by birds, all these would probably sprout at a similar rate to my planted seeds, assuming the soil was in a favorable condition to nourish my planted seeds. When my planted seeds had taken hold and were clearly visible I would do a *thorough* weeding. This would give the plants I wanted a head start over the weeds.

After that point I would weed within the row (between the plants in the row) quite thoroughly, and make it a rule that the weeds in between the rows should never get bigger than my cultivated plants, and should *never go to seed*. This is *not* a system of "clean cultivation." Clean cultivation is where weeds are *kept out* of the garden. They are removed as soon as they appear. Gardening by mulching (that is, covering the ground except for the plants you want) is a system of clean cultivation: the only plants that are *allowed to grow* are the cultivated plants. The system I proposed would be absolutely disastrous unless there were some way the weeds removed could be returned to the garden in a "harmless" (or rather, useful!) state—as nutritive material for building up the soil. The way I proposed to return the weeds, with their naturally corrective qualities to my soil, was to compost them.

Composting is a natural process by which certain bacteria decompose organic matter into humus, the life-giving substance in the soil. The bacteria that do this occur naturally in the soil. So what I would do would be to pile the *healthy* weeds (always destroying diseased plants separately) I pulled out of my garden on some exposed ground, periodically sprinkling them with dirt (to supply the bacteria); I would also put all kitchen wastes on this pile, as well as any inedible parts of all healthy cultivated plants. When the bacteria had done their job, I would use this "compost" as fertilizer. That way whatever came out of the soil would go back in. But what about the stuff we ate? Westerners have a thing about not using human manure for vegetable growing. I myself prefer a septic tank to an outhouse to be shoveled out onto a compost pile. So I decided to use surrogate manure. I would use horse, cow, sheep and chicken manure where available and sprinkle this in layers on the compost pile.

Another fundamental principle I would apply would be crop rotation. I would not plant the same type of plant in the same location two years in a row. Then the soil would actually improve over successive gardening years, and there is less of a chance of plant disease and parasites "digging in" specific to any particular plant. It is a matter of hygiene as well as of nutrition.

As for insects, I would learn to recognize a few of the more obnoxious garden pests, keep an eye out for them and hand-pick them or their egg clusters where necessary. If an infestation seemed likely to get out of hand, I would sprinkle individual plants with wood ashes, a simple and harmless remedy for many insect problems. If a season showed me that bugs were a real problem, then the following spring I would order praying mantis eggs and lady bugs from Sears or Ward's and scatter them around the garden. (Praying mantises will eat anything that moves—including praying mantises—with the exception of ants.)

My main remedy for insect pests would be birds. I would encourage birds in my garden unless they proved to me they would eat the seed and young plants instead of the insects. I would, of course, be sure to cover the seed well and pat down firmly so the rain would not wash the soil off and expose them. (Since I probably won't get back to this, let me say that I have lost no plants, or parts of plants to birds. Since I have very few insect problems, I suspect that I owe the birds a large vote of thanks!) But it must be kept in mind that much of the land around here is wild, so the birds have excellent alternative sources of seed, fruit and sprouts of various sorts. My garden supplies what they don't have much of—some open dirt area from which to gather insects! People in more suburban or more intensively cultivated settings may have a different experience and lose some early produce off their plants.

So far I have been talking organic gardening—my own personal brand of organic gardening. (There are many versions. My father, for instance, who gardens organically, does not approve of my position on weeds.) But while organic gardening was my preference for health and aesthetic reasons, I decided I would not be fanatical on the subject. For instance, much of the commercially available seed is treated with various poisons, including mercury, which can be quite deadly! This treatment supposedly guards the seed until it gets a chance to germinate, and makes it resistant to certain diseases. It is possible to locate sources of untreated seed, but there were decided advantages to using the treated seed available locally. I didn't like the idea of treated seed, but I needed to be able to browse through packages of seed to decide as I went along what I would plant in my garden. I didn't even know how big my first garden would be, or when it would be ready for planting, or how long the local growing season was—or, for that matter, how we'd get the garden plowed.

I eventually located a source of seeds which were not treated (see Sources for Supplies at the end of the book for details). Where it was a simple thing to do, I would keep my own seed. This can get complicated. Some desirable varieties are hybrids that don't breed true. Other plants take a couple of years to go to seed. So that little extra psychological space I gained that first year by using locally available seed was more valuable to me than a rigid stance on organic principles.

I also decided that I wouldn't start plants going indoors the first year or two. House plants and I don't mix somehow. But the season is too short here to grow things like tomatoes outdoors from seed, so I decided to buy tomato "sets" (small plants you set out) and cabbage and onion plants from a nursery. The chances were that sets grown in local nurseries would not have been started using organic gardening techniques.

Another exception to my organic gardening plan was the matter of manure. Since I had not gardened here before, I did not have a compost pile. I didn't have animals. I didn't have a barn or any ready composted manure lying around. This meant that I had to buy composted manure. (Fresh manure is too strong and will burn plants.) I knew very well that the bagged manure available in stores comes from dairy farms, and while the manure is well composted, the cattle that produce the manure are not necessarily fed food grown by organic methods. Not only that, the cattle may well have been dosed up with drugs and hormones, traces of which might show up in the manure. I needed to use manure because the garden area had been worked

before, probably for a long time, and I had no idea of how
seriously previous occupants had taken the notion of crop
rotation.

There was another question I decided to ignore, unless
it proved necessary to take it into account: soil acidity. Many
garden vegetables don't like a very acid soil. I decided to
plant and see what happened—if my plants didn't grow, I'd
get into soil testing. (Gardening stores sell kits for determining soil acidity, complete with information about how much,
if any, lime you need to neutralize excess acidity. I've never
used such a kit. My garden grows well, so I don't bother.)

So all that was the theory. Now, here's what I do.

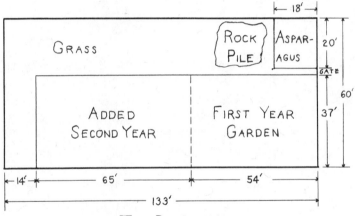

THE BIG GARDEN

*The first-year garden provided all our vegetables for the
summer, plus a few cabbages and squash for the winter. The
following year we added a 410-square-foot spring garden
elsewhere, and extended the big garden as you can see. This
virtually provided year-round vegetables. Next year we'll start
planting the grassy areas, too. We've put sheep fence around the
whole thing. We use the area as a winter barnyard, getting
manure on the garden without work.*

Plowing the Garden

Luckily I started with an area that had been gardened. It was neglected, true, but it had been a garden, which was testified to by the huge rock pile next to it. We live on a mountain, and mountains are known for their rocks! It wasn't the best garden situation in the world . . . that was for sure . . . along the bottom edge of the garden runs a swampy belt, so the garden cannot be called well drained. But the soil is good, and if the frost heaves up more rocks, well, so the rocks will get dug out. If I had to wait a little bit longer before the plot changed back from mud into soil each spring, well, it would also mean that I would have fewer watering problems later in the season. It was my garden, and I was prepared to love it.

April went by. May went by. In the beginning of June, I pronounced my garden ready for working. It finally passed the moisture test I had imposed on it every few days for the past weeks. The test was simple. I would scoop up a handful of soil, squeeze it in my hand, and let go. If I gave the mound a light tap and it crumbled, it was ready. If it stayed in one piece, or only broke in half, it was too wet. This test worked for me the three years I've had a garden. The first year, Mel's cousin very kindly rototilled our garden for use. The soil was in perfect condition for working—it crumbled nicely when rototilled. A friend and neighbor bought a tractor and offered to plow for us the second year.

When he plowed, the earth fell from the plow and crumbled nicely. Even in the sod area he plowed for me, the earth on the sods powdered nicely. He was half convinced I had been right to wait. He became even more convinced when his wife tried to plant her garden. It had become compacted from too early plowing. She complained she couldn't even get a pickax into it to dig a hole for her tomato plants. I tried it, and she was right. She redid half her garden with the aid of our rototiller and a lot of sweat, then finally, as even that was not a satisfactory solution, had him plow it again. Luckily, this time, the soil loosened up and all was well. I say luckily, because my father from Texas tells me that he's seen land that was so badly compacted from too early plowing that it took years for the clods to break up! SO DON'T WORK THE SOIL WHILE IT IS SOGGY, OR YOU WILL BE SORRY!

The purpose of plowing, or rototilling, or spading, is to loosen the soil up and get some air into it so the plants can breathe and send their roots deep and far in search of nourishment. Plowing is all you need for some crops: corn, potatoes, transplants (see next chapter for details). But for fine seeds, the garden needs more preparation.

Preparing a Seed Bed

What I do is this—I take a garden fork and "work" down the row. A garden fork is a heavy-tined fork with a three-foot handle. I work backwards, so I don't have to walk on an area I've forked over. I push the fork in (using my foot for extra force) as far as I can, lift up some earth and shake it off the fork. I remove any largish rocks, glass, old bedsprings and whatever else turns up. I also remove all the weed roots I find. When I've done the whole row, I walk around the garden (never walk in the garden more than you have to, it packs down the earth, especially in the first stages), and rake across the row I've just forked over. I rake out all the smaller stones which might interfere with the small seeds I will be planting. This is called preparing the seed bed.

When that's done, I set up a garden line. A garden line is a piece of twine tied to stakes at each end. I drive a stake in at one end of the row, walk around the garden and drive in the other stake at the opposite end. Then I twist the stakes until the line is good and taut. A garden line is *very* important. Straight rows make life a lot easier later on, let me tell you! (Use white twine. I found a neighbor going half blind trying to use dark green string.) Then I get my seed packet, a pan of composted manure, and I'm ready to plant.

How to Plant Seeds

Medium-sized seeds I plant as follows: I squat down and draw a line in the earth with my finger. I sprinkle on some composted manure, then place (not pour) the seeds appropriately. Seeds that are small, but not outrageously small, I treat as follows: I pour some from the envelope into one hand. Then I pick up a few with the thumb and index finger of the other hand, and sprinkle them *sparsely* along the row. Outrageously small seed I first mix carefully with some fine earth, I sprinkle the mixture along the row. This makes it a lot easier to get an even seeding. After I have placed the seeds as far as I can reach from one position, I brush the earth over them and pat it down firmly so the seed won't wash away. Then I take a big step and do the next section of row.

When the whole row is finished, I leave the garden line where it was and fork over the next strip (where I'd been standing to plant before, in fact). I rake it over, and then move the garden line. By forking as I go along, I ensure that all the areas I've walked on have been loosened up again. When I move the garden line, I make sure to mark the row I've finished with stakes, and I keep a record of what's where in a notebook. That's all there is to seeding.

The mistakes a beginner is most likely to make are: not getting the soil loose enough; seeding too heavily; not patting down the planted seed firmly enough; giving in to a desire to "use up" the whole envelope of seeds. *Never, ever* pour seed out of the envelope, even if the instructions tell you to. It takes quite a knack to do it right.

For your first garden, follow the instructions on the seed package as to spacing. After you've seen the plants at all stages of growth, you might want to modify those instructions . . . like putting the rows closer together, or something of the sort.

A city type who has never seen common vegetables growing will be shocked by the size of many garden plants. If you are buying young plants to transplant into your garden, ask the person at the nursery to tell you how far apart to put that variety, and how deep to set it in. And if he or she says, "Oh, about a foot apart," show them with your hands what you think a foot is. Chances are they'll gesture a correction with their hands . . . and give a different spacing entirely. Go by the gesture, not the number. And work out a rule of thumb for yourself. Measure the various joints of your fingers, your arm, to find out what's an inch, half an inch, a foot, a yard, and so on. Mark off your rake handle in the most common dimensions for row widths. Whenever you move the garden line, use these marks as guides. And by the way, we've heard that it's a good idea to leave the handles of your tools unpainted. The paint blisters after a while, making them very hard on the hands.

Mel's father gave us a piece of advice that is invaluable, although it does not seem so at first hearing. "Never walk out of the garden empty-handed," he said. "Always carry out a rock, some weeds, or some glass." Follow this advice and work will get itself done. It is also based on another very important premise: Don't walk on the garden unnecessarily, especially when the ground is wet. It compacts the soil and makes for extra hard work. Once the garden is planted, *stay out of it* until it is time for the first weeding and thinning.

Which brings me to the new gardener's greatest fear: how to tell the cultivated plants from the weeds.

Actually, it is easy. That's one good reason to plant in straight rows. When the plants first come up, stand at the edge and squint. First of all, the weeds will be a somewhat different color in the row. If you are in doubt about whether a certain plant is a weed or a vegetable, look elsewhere in the garden to see if it is growing there, too. If it is, chances are it is a weed. If it isn't, it might be what you planted. If it is that hard to tell, wait another couple of days and look again. When weeding early in the season, hold down the plants you want while you pull the weeds in the row so you don't accidentally dislodge your wanted plants.

If you are not lucky enough to have a site that already has been gardened, and you don't have access to a plow or a rototiller, you probably first will have to remove the sod. Sod is a layer of grass and roots like a carpet. To remove it, mark out strips or squares by whacking straight down hard with the broad blade of a mattock (a cross between a pick-axe and a hoe). When all sides of the piece to be removed are cut through, whack the broad blade of the mattock under one edge and pull up. Mel says, "It rolls right up." What he means is, with a great deal of labor and sweat in the eyes, you will manage to dislodge it and roll up the sod. When you discover how heavy sod is, you will unroll it and cut it in small chunks. The sod, of course, goes on the compost pile (upside down, so it doesn't keep growing). You want all that good topsoil back for next year's garden.

Speaking of compost piles, I said that all kitchen refuse, weedy stuff, hunks of sod, and unused parts of plants go on the compost pile. There is more to it than that. It is not enough just to throw the stuff in a heap on the grass somewhere. I know because we tried it. The organic materials to be composted should be in contact with the earth so that the proper bacteria can get working. What we ended up doing was removing an oblong area of sod and building a frame around the bared ground, made of old window screens (held together with hooks and eyes so they may be easily moved or removed as necessary). This is our compost pile. Actually, I have three of these bins going. Every few inches of height of garbage and weeds should be covered with a sprinkling of soil (an inch or less), and manure if you can get it. This provides the necessary bacteria, and, incidentally, keeps odors and flies from gathering. Then another layer of garbagey stuff, and so on. The piles should be watered periodically in dry weather, and holes poked in it so air can get through (the bacteria need the air to work properly). If possible, the whole pile should be turned periodically. At the end of a season it may be topped off with manure and a layer of sod, if that's handy, or dirt. Wood ash is a very good ingredient in compost piles. Water leaches lye out of the wood ash and hastens the decomposition process, and incidentally corrects any tendency toward too great acidity. The compost pile does not smell bad, and if it is kept covered does not attract insects or animals. It should be properly composted within a year or two, depending on how good you are about watering and turning it.

Some people keep a compost pile only during the summer. During the winter they dump kitchen refuse, leaves, etc., right in the garden to be plowed under in the spring. This is advisable only if you and your neighbors don't have free running dogs, though, because grease, meat scraps and old bones are all irresistible.

There are faster methods of making compost, involving either dumping lye over it or adding a bacterial starter, or both, and turning it frequently. We have not tried these methods, however. A good gardening store should have further information. Some people use half composted materials as mulch: they spread it around plants a couple of inches deep to keep weeds from growing up. The bottom layer rots and becomes fertilizer. What may *not* be done with any hope of success is to keep taking nutrients out of the soil without putting some back.

If you have an old barn on your property, you will probably have a manure pile or dirty stall you can raid for your first year's supply of fertilizer. Or turn up someone who does have one and offer to clean the stable. Fresh manure, however, should not be used when planting the garden; as I have mentioned, it burns young plants. The manure should be one, or preferably two years old. Properly composted manure has no odor, and is not unpleasant to handle.

There are things which decompose very slowly: hair, bones, corn stalks, twiggy stuff and brush. If they are to be used in the compost pile, either chop them up in a "mulcher" or set up a separate pile for them (it makes it a lot easier to turn the pile). They'll take a bit longer to decompose.

When the garden is finished for the year, we pull out everything inedible and put it on the compost pile. Then we till the garden and spread leaves over the area of garden we will want to work soonest (a few inches of leaves over the entire garden keeps it in better condition for the spring: the frost doesn't go as deep, for one thing). Most of the leaves should be removed before plowing, but I leave a few since I have very heavy soil and it loosens up a bit if some leaves are chopped in. If you are going in for mulch gardening, which I don't do, you can just pull aside the leaves for planting the next season, leaving them in piles between the rows to shade out the weeds. If you do this, however, be conscientious about bug-picking, since many night-feeding bugs hide in mulch during hot days.

By the way, what with fuel crises and all, organic gardening is a very good skill to learn. Some ingredients of commercial fertilizers require the use of fossil fuels, and are becoming very expensive and rather scarce. As prices go up more people do home gardening, so get your seed as early in the season as you can manage to avoid disappointment. Pick varieties that suit your growing season (ask the neighbors). Around here the growing season is *very* short, so I have to choose varieties that mature quickly, even at the expense of a large yield. The date from planting to maturity should be marked on the seed packet for that variety.

Greer in the Garden

I called this chapter the gardening passion. For me that's what it is. I am happiest when I am in the garden. During the summer I get what I call "antzy" if I don't spend a few minutes each morning wandering around the garden inspecting the plants. When I'm in the garden my head gets quiet inside . . . I don't even hear the traffic on Route 43 anymore. If Mel wants me, he really has to work hard to get my attention. Time passes calmly, and I am in a state of perfect contentment. And if I can find time actually to sit and stare at the garden for a while each day, then everyone in the family is happier, since I am, too.

It is a totally new kind of experience for me. In fact, I was afraid it might wear off when the novelty wore off. But with my second garden the contentment and calm increased even over the first year, since I realized that everything—or most everything—would in fact grow. I feel secure when I'm fussing with a vegetable garden. Not so with flowers. Every so often I try to grow some flowers, and each time I get frustrated and impatient. It is only vegetable gardening that does this for me. Obviously, a garden is very little work if one has this gardening passion.

By the way, there is a lot of chance to work out frustrations in gardening. When I really get mad at something or someone, I go out and bug-pick. I was rather squeamish about bug-picking until I realized what good therapy it could be. See that green worm on the cabbage? Here's one for big business (squnch). Here's one for that secretary at college who wouldn't let me use the elevator when I was fainting (squish), and so it goes. And after the row of cabbage is done, well, I feel better. And if you like to read really gory bedtime stories, try some of the books on garden pests. They make spy thrillers look tame.

Mel in the Garden

Mel is different. He doesn't enjoy the picky little stuff that has to be done in the garden, like weeding, or thinning, or even harvesting (although he did dig the potatoes for me, and it is his job to pick the sweet corn). But Mel really enjoys using efficient, effective machines. I don't (except for typewriters and mimeograph machines). I resent noise in the garden; Mel thrives on it. So Mel and I were both overjoyed when Mel's father gave us a rototiller last Christmas. A rototiller is the home gardener's substitute for a plow. It is like a walking lawn mower, except that it has teeth that churn up the soil for planting. With a lot of going back and forth it will even churn up sod. And it can be used for cultivating . . . that is, weeding between the rows. The outer two teeth come off so it can be run down a relatively narrow row. It is very fast, and can do a good job. If you can't get your garden plowed, try to beg, borrow or rent one of these very useful machines when first putting in your garden. It makes life a lot simpler. If you are going to buy, and can afford it, get a Troybuilt. They are easy to manage, extremely efficient, and parts are readily available. They are well worth the extra expense.

For cultivating even narrower rows than a rototiller can get through, we have a push cultivator. It consists of two long, waist-length handles attached at the bottom to a single wheel with a claw. One wheels it down the row to scratch out weeds and loosen the ground. It does a row in about two minutes. Mel's father picked up a used one for us. If you can't find a used one, Sears and Wards sell them in their farm catalogs.

Miriam in the Garden

I didn't let little Miriam into the garden until the plants were nearly full grown. Then I would occasionally take her in (she was a year and a half old by that time), carefully pointing out the little paths between the rows, and the different plants. She developed a passion for fresh onions, so I would pull them for her to munch on. I showed her the most common weed in the garden, told her it was a weed, and let her do a little weeding "like Mommy," every once in a while. She considered it a great privilege, and did a pretty good job of weeding the onions. The main thing was to keep her in an area where the plant she was pulling was enormously different from the vegetables in the row. Miriam is very interested in this world of ours, and any information one can give her is highly appreciated. She also has a delight in doing the same things adults do. I let her plant one hill of pole beans; Mel set the pole and I drew a circle around it. We showed her how to sprinkle manure along the drill, then poke holes and put beans in each hole, and cover them up. She patted them down very carefully indeed.

Another job in Miriam's life is harvesting. Mommy pulls the onions, or daddy digs the potatoes, and Miriam carries each one (one at a time) to a bushel basket. Less fortunate was her discovery that she could pull string beans off the row of bush beans all by herself. Unfortunately, she didn't yet have the coordination to do it without pulling down the plants, too. She also liked to pull carrots and beets when the ground was soft, but found it frustrating when they were "too stuck," as she put it. I sympathized, since I, too, get frustrated when they are too stuck.

The decision to let Miriam into the garden was carefully thought out. I didn't want her growing up hating the garden because it kept me so busy during certain seasons. Certainly, if I wanted her help later on, she must develop pleasant associations with it now, so a lot of yelling or cringing on my part every time she made a mistake would be worse than keeping her out altogether. It required a lot of patience and self-control on my part, since I get very attached to my plants, but worked out very well. She became a real help.

CHAPTER 5

GETTING IT ALL IN: RECIPES FOR PLANTING, HARVESTING, AND USING GARDEN FRESH VEGETABLES

Greer speaking

A woman I know who has a summer house in the country, but who has to return to the suburbs during the school year, told me she'd love to have a garden but she does not have enough time at her country home to benefit by one. "I'd have to leave before harvest time, so there's no point. I do grow a few tomatoes, but that's it." This is utter nonsense. Certainly some things, like cabbage, do a lot of their growing well into cold weather, but many things are harvested and used all during the summer.

We start eating salads and greens (especially chard) within two weeks of planting. Beets can be eaten at any stage of growth. And you can pull carrots any time—if they are not gigantic, all the better. They'll be sweeter. Beans and zucchini planted in June are at their peak at the beginning of August. And so it goes. I suspect that woman just doesn't like gardening.

The bulk of the harvesting process *must* occur during the course of the summer. Summer squash gets tough and seedy if left on the vine too long. Beans and peas get tough, starchy, and dry out if not picked regularly. Greens get tough and go to seed if not cut periodically. And the rule seems to be in gardening that the more and sooner you pick, the more you get. If the plant does not have to support mature fruit, it makes new ones.

Of course there does come a time when the garden is finishing up for the year—around here it is frost dependent —and things must be gotten in for the winter. It's a lot of work, but in sheer bulk it is a mere fraction of what is brought in and consumed (and processed) during the course of the summer! And the vacation gardener can dispense with many of the fall vegetables if time is a problem . . . the garden will still be a profitable endeavor!

I'll talk about the things I plant in my garden, how I plant them, how I care for them, what they look like when they come from the garden, and how I use them. I'll talk in detail about storing them for winter in a series of separate chapters to follow, but will indicate here what methods are appropriate to each vegetable.

I plan my garden in terms of seasonal use, so I'll tell about it that way. My main garden is too muddy for very early planting, but I have a small patch elsewhere which drains out a month earlier than the big garden does. I call it my spring garden. I devote it to things that are somewhat frost resistant, but which do poorly in hot weather. When the spring garden is in, and the main garden drains out, I plant part of the main garden to frost-resistant things for early summer menus. When all danger of frost is past, I set out the frost-sensitive vegetables for my summer garden. When these are all in I start planting for fall use: vegetables which are frost-resistant, and store well in the root cellar. And here is how it all works . . .

The Spring Garden

LETTUCE: I plant loose-leaf lettuce rather than head lettuce. I only had leaf lettuce once in the city—my grocer never got it in again, since the extremely tender loose-leaf lettuce *doesn't* travel well, while head lettuce can take quite a beating before it gets rotten through. Everyone else I know also grows loose-leaf lettuce, possibly because when one has a garden one tends to develop a fresh-from-the-garden fetish. With me it has become a full-fledged prejudice. I find it actually *impossible* to use produce I've stored a day or so in the refrigerator. I give it away or put it in the compost heap or give it to the chickens. It just seems silly to eat even day-old produce when I can wander out to the garden half an hour or so before dinner and pick what I need for a meal. When the garden is finished for the season, I revert to my city habits and serve stored produce without any problem at all, so fortunately it is just a summer prejudice. But my salads are gorgeous because of it, I'm convinced.

I usually plant two or three varieties of loose-leaf lettuce (they all taste and look quite different), and mix them in salads. I've grown black-seeded Simpson, salad bowl lettuce, oak leaf lettuce, and romaine lettuce. If I were only to grow one type, I would choose either black-seeded Simpson or salad bowl lettuce, as these are the most delicately flavored and finely textured. Flavor can be added by throwing some beet thinnings or chard thinnings in with it. Romaine, it turns out, doesn't like hot weather (it goes to seed) and the thinnings are tough, so if you put it in, set it out in your first planting and don't bother with it for midsummer. I love the oak leaf lettuce, and would certainly suggest it as a second lettuce. Its leaves are shaped like oak leaves. It has a strong taste, is rather crunchy, and doubles very nicely as a cooked green (if you like cooked escarole, you'll like cooked oak leaf lettuce; it has a mild dandelion green flavor). Speaking of escarole, I plant it in midsummer for late fall use.

Planting lettuce: Lettuce seed is small, but not outrageously tiny, so I draw a shallow line and use the thumb–index-finger sprinkling technique, first sprinkling composted manure or compost along the row. It seems to take a week for the tiny lettuce leaves to appear (if the soil and weather condition is right, that is. Any seed will rot out if it is planted in mud). The little leaves are light green, so are easily distinguishable from weeds. When they are large enough to handle, (this will be obvious—they get a couple of inches high and you can begin telling one plant from another) it's time for the first weeding and thinning. Thin the lettuce right into the salad bowl. Continue thinning for use whenever the plants look crowded, pulling out the weakest plants (i.e., the smallest). The idea is that no two plants should be coming out of the same hole, so to speak (again this will make sense when you see it). As the tops get bigger and the stems thicker, I thin again. When the plants are big and properly spaced, I begin cutting rather than pulling.

There are two styles of harvesting mature loose-leaf lettuce. One way is to cut individual large leaves off the plant, leaving the small ones to develop. But I prefer to cut the whole plant (I use a small paring knife and cut slightly above ground level). The stem soon begins making new leaves for a second and third harvest. This method has the advantage of keeping the lettuce plant from going to seed so quickly. I usually cut alternate plants to keep the row looking pretty and thriving, but that's window (salad?) dressing.

There is a non-thinning technique for growing loose-leaf lettuce. *If* you've succeeded in seeding sparsely, you just let the plants fight it out among themselves. From the time they are two or three inches high, cut along the row with a paring knife as much as you want for a meal. The hardier plants will sprout new leaves and force the smaller ones out. I've done it both ways, and I've found that the no-thinning approach works well as long as there are good growing conditions. But come a catastrophe, like a hail storm or tornado (both of which we've had here, one each year), the plants that were thinned recovered much faster, while the plants that were not thinned required a lot of care before they revived. If you haven't thinned, and a catastrophe comes, let the plants alone for a day to see if they'll perk up on their own. If they do, leave them alone. If they don't, go down the row and thin, leaving the healthiest-looking plants with lots of breathing space. Also weed thoroughly and remove any leaves that are actually rotting. The extra room will bring the plants around within a few days. Also, if you have a period of extended drought and can't water the garden, do the same: get those weeds out, every one of them, and thin the plants. This goes for any garden plant, not only for lettuce.

I rarely have to make a project of weeding in the lettuce row. I make it a matter of policy to weed a little whenever I harvest. That extra five minutes here and there does wonders. I do have to weed between the rows periodically (say a couple of times a month). I do this by either whacking between the rows with a hoe to loosen up the soil and get the weeds out, or running down the row with my little Greer-powered cultivator. It takes a very few minutes per row.

Plant at least two, better three, plantings of lettuce. Some people plant every two weeks, but I find once a month just about right. After a while lettuce goes to seed, especially in hot weather. The "heart" of the lettuce will begin lengthening out into a stalk, with the leaves growing out at intervals from it. It's actually very pretty: it makes a sort of ruffly cone. After a while it will make flowers. At this point the lettuce turns bitter, so have the next batch ready to use. Pull the plants and give them to the chickens; cook them as greens; give them to the neighbors; or make lettuce soap from them. Or throw them on the compost pile and scatter some turnip seed in the row for an additional crop out of that row.

Using garden fresh lettuce: Home grown lettuce can be quite gritty. Before I got the hang of washing it, I would spend forty-five minutes cleaning and still end up with grit in the salad. Now I gather the lettuce half an hour or so before we want to make the salad, cut out the "heart," and put it and the lettuce leaves in very cold water for fifteen minutes or so. The grit soaks off and sinks to the bottom of the bowl. I lift the leaves out of the water, letting them drain for a moment, then dip them a few times in fresh water to get out any grit that might have settled on the leaves. I clean the "hearts" separately by spraying them with the kitchen spray. Then I pick over the leaves for bad spots and bugs. (We seem to miss one green worm or slug a year, although it is possible that we have eaten a few others that we didn't see. Garden bugs seem cleaner than city roaches, somehow, *if* you don't spray, that is.)

ONIONS: Since I didn't grow enough onions for winter use last year, I went to our local farm stand in the autumn and bought three fifty-pound sacks of small (not tiny, just small) onions. (They cost half the price of the big ones—I paid something like $2.50 a bag for them.) Three sacks were way too many, and come spring I had fifty pounds of onions left over, many of them gaily sprouting through the holes in the trash burner we stored them in. I gave away as many as I could, made piles of onion soup, creamed onions and what not, but still had some left. So I sorted out the onions that had begun sprouting and planted them in my little spring garden. I just poked a stick in the ground to make a hole, dropped in some composted manure, stuck in the onion, leaving the green sticking out, and firmed the earth, then went on to the next. I put them very close together, almost touching, since I would be pulling them for use from day to day. Within a week the pale yellow "greens" had greened and firmed up, and were growing into beautiful scallions. I began thinning for use almost immediately, and by the time I had gone around the little garden once, some of the onions I'd left in were beginning to split, that is, the old bulb was dividing into two brand new bulbs. I could tell the old bulbs were splitting because two bunches of greens would be growing out of the one bulb. So for a second crop, I held down the base of the plant with one hand, and with the other hand I pulled out the smaller bunch of greens. A little onion would come out with it. (If the ground is loose, as it should be in a properly tended garden, the second plant will pull right out of the onion skin.) Then I tucked back the earth around the plant that remained so it had room to grow into a nice big onion for me.

Even in my big garden, I plant "sets" rather than onion seed. I have a short growing season, and I've heard that growing onions from seed is a nuisance. Sets are tiny onion bulbs that were grown from seed the previous year, but not allowed to grow big. I plant them the way I planted the onions in my spring garden, close together, and thin them for use. The first year, I planted one pound of yellow onion sets, just about enough to last through the summer. This year, I planted yellow onions sets, more sets from the winter storage supply, and two pounds of white onion sets. These are beautiful tasting onions, so plant some by all means!

Onions reproduce in two ways. Sometimes the bulbs split, as I mentioned. Sometimes, during the growing season, a tough stalk will appear in the midst of the tender onion greens. On top of this stalk, or a little way down, a little turban will form, resembling the turrets on the Kremlin. This is the flower bud. I let some go to see what happens, and it eventually opens up into a really exquisite flower. However, good gardening practice says don't let this happen. But opinions differ on what is to be done about it.

Some people say just pinch the buds off (they're strong —use them in soups and stews) and let the plants be. Eventually the greens will drop over and dry up of their own accord.

Some people say pinch the buds off and "lay the greens down."

Some people say leave the buds on, but roll down the row with a barrel, or something heavy, or trample the greens down.

One man stopped by and told me to "whack off the greens with a machete."

I've tried all these approaches, plus letting the onions do their thing without interference. The onions do get bigger if you pinch off the buds before they make flowers. As far as "laying the greens down" is concerned, I find they just stand right up again, even if I pinch the base of the stem firmly. The same goes for trampling them down; indeed, if the buds are not broken off they will open even if in a prone condition. As for whacking with a machete, well, I didn't use a machete. With a paring knife I cut some onion greens for creamed onion greens and vichyssoise; I don't like this technique at all, although I did like the creamed onion greens and the vichyssoise. I had to bend the stumps down again and again so water would not collect in the hollow leaves and rot out the onion. So next year, I'll just pinch off the buds and have done with it. Try them all. Maybe you'll be able to trample, whack, or "lay them down" more effectively than I. I must admit my heart wasn't in all these things, since I like to see nice healthy onion greens greeting the sun.

Using garden fresh onions: Luckily, Mel's mother was around the first time I pulled an onion from the garden, or else I might have thrown out the whole row! I was convinced that my onion was the victim of some disease. You know the nice, shiny, dry onion skin of the store-bought onion? Well, that is thick and spongy and mushy and rotten-looking while the onion is growing. Surprised at my gasp of horror as I looked at the messy object, Mel's mother said, "They're *supposed* to be like that!" She pulled the slimy part of it off (no tearful peeling operation), and there beneath was a sound, beautiful scallion (it was early in the season and I was thinning for use). It wasn't disease after all.

The first year my onions were so strong as to be absolutely raucous. I complained about this to a veteran gardener, and he told me the secret of sweet onions. If the bulb sticks out of the ground as it is growing, the sun will make it very strong. So for sweet onions, I had only to go down the row once in a while and whack the dirt over the bulbs (called hilling up). This blanches them nicely and they come out mild and sweet. I do some both ways, now, since I like both strong and sweet onions.

After the greens have completely died down, the onions are ready for final harvesting. I go down the row and pull up those I see. The first year, unfortunately, I left it at that, but this year I found out purely by accident that frequently the onion bulb has split and the smaller bulb does not always pull up with the big bulb. So now, after I pull the onions I see, I dig down the row with a garden fork and get a bonus crop of little onions.

Onions may be stored in a root celler and may be dried, canned or pickled.

GARLIC: I grow garlic the same way I grow onions. Separate the bulb of garlic into individual cloves (don't peel them, though) and plant the cloves, pointed side up. *Don't* plant them in an area of garden which is likely to have grassy weeds, though, because the thin fronds of the garlic look just like the blades of grass, and make weeding very frustrating indeed. You don't discover you've pulled a garlic plant out until you get that lovely garlic aroma. For early use, just snip off the garlic greens as you need them. They are milder than the bulbs. Since they are not hollow like onion greens, there is no danger of the bulbs collecting water and rotting when snipped. Toward midsummer, thin them for use. We chop the whole cluster (the papery stuff surrounding each clove has not developed yet). At the end of the summer we dig them like onions. Cooking with fresh garlic is a truly enlightening experience.

Many people plant garlic near their tomatoes to discourage bugs.

One family has a garlic patch they let run wild. Every fall they dig up what they'll need for the winter, and let the rest stay in the ground to make more garlic for the following year. Don't let it or onions go wild anywhere near where milk animals graze, however, or you'll be sorry. Both onions and garlic come through in the milk. I'm convinced that's why Miriam likes onions and garlic so much. She's had them from birth.

Garlic is a plant with many virtues, aside from its warm, hearty flavor. A French woman taught my mother to make up a real garlicky soup and feed it to the family whenever colds or flus are going around. My M.D. godfather (Hun-

garian) informed us that garlic has mild antibiotic qualities.
I've recently heard rumors that garlic keeps down the tendency toward cholesterol buildup in arteries, so whether for
health or for taste, grow it by all means.

PEAS: I was determined to grow peas in my first year
garden. But when the garden finally got ready for planting,
Mel's mother told me it was too late. "We always said peas
by the Fourth of July," she told me, since peas don't do well
in very hot weather. This past year, however, I decided to
put a short row of peas in my tiny spring garden to see how
they would do. I planted them in May, and did get peas for
the Fourth of July, in fact, a few before, and, of course, more
after that. This is a vegetable that city people *can't* experience properly.

There are two types of pea plants: dwarf and climbing
peas. I put in the dwarf peas this year because I didn't want
to mess with chicken wire trellises for the peas to climb up.
But the vines flopped over and it was very hard to pick and
to weed, so next year I will give them support. I'll get Mel
to tack chicken wire to some stakes and set them up for me,
and I'll plant a row to climb up each side.

Pea plants are beautiful—delicate looking and graceful.
First they make little rounded leaves from off their stalks,
with tendrils that grab on to any stray weed (so weed them
thoroughly when they're little, or you'll have problems!).
Then they make flattish white flowers, and eventually a pea
pod peeks out of the flower, and the flower withers and the
pea pod begins to develop. If you've planted an "edible pod"
or snow pea, you have to watch carefully and pick off the
little pods almost as soon as they form, so they don't get tough
and stringy. If you've planted ordinary peas, however, wait
until the pods "flesh out," but be sure not to let them go too
long. Pick over the row every day or two and you'll have
sweet peas. Let them go just a couple of days too long and

they'll be starchy, like the ones you get in the city. I love to eat fresh peas raw, so I never did cook any sweet peas this year. While peas were in season, I'd go pick over the row every day and we'd sit outside before dinner and shell them and eat them. They were our delectable *hors d'oeuvres,* and disgustingly healthy. Country life tends to be that way. The pea pods may be thrown into the stock pot, cooked until they've given up their juice, then discarded.

Come hot weather, the peas stop producing much. They'll make occasional pods, but are not as tasty as the early ones. At this point, I let them go. Once every week or so I look over the plants for pods that are drying out, and pick these and spread them out in the shed to dry some more. I shell them and use them for ham bone soup, the way you use split peas. If you have lots of vines, and have eaten, canned and frozen what you want of them in their green state, then let the plants go until they are covered with mature pods, pull the whole plants and hang them in bunches in a shed somewhere until they dry out. For more details, see Drying.

WARNING: Never ever cook dried peas or dried beans in a pressure cooker!!! It clogs the vents and messes up the safety valves and could explode!!! The warning does not, however, apply to *canning* dried beans or peas when they are enclosed in jars. It applies to cooking them loose, not in containers, in a pressure cooker.

The Early Summer Garden

When the big garden is ready for planting, but there is still danger of frost (not when there *will* be frost, when there *might* be frost) I put in early plantings of the following vegetables, which can stand a little frost if they have to:

BEETS: Beet seeds are easily manageable in size. Actually, though, what you take out of the seed envelope is really a cluster of seeds rather than a single seed, so they have to be planted rather more sparsely than one might imagine. I plant them about an inch apart (draw the line, sprinkle in manure, then seed, cover and pat down). Beets are a good thing for a beginning gardener to grow, since they are an obviously different color from any weeds likely to spring up in the row. As soon as they are big enough so that I can tell one plant from another, I thin them (into the salad bowl . . . and is that ever a good salad!). As usual, no plants coming out of the same hole are permitted. Then I wait until the beets are as big as my fingernail and do another thinning. This time I cook them whole . . . tops and roots, a really superb treat. I continue thinning for use whenever they look crowded, or whenever I want to serve beets. I weed when the row looks weedy, and loosen up the soil between the row once or twice a month.

Occasionally a leaf hopper will eat a tiny hole in a beet green. Since the beet plants don't seem to worry about them, I don't either. When the beets are big, I cook beets and tops separately, treating the tops like spinach. Most of the new gardeners I've met develop a passion for beet greens very quickly. Old timers don't need their taste developed; they have it already.

Beets are *significantly* different stored and fresh-picked. Fresh pulled beets are *really* sweet, so try growing some, even if city beets never seemed enticing.

Pull beets to harvest. Cut off the greens, leaving an inch or two of stem so the beet root doesn't "bleed" when cooked. Beets need vigorous scrubbing with a vegetable brush, with special attention paid to the tops. Greens should be soaked for a few minutes in very cold water, then the leaves lifted in and out of fresh water a few times to remove dirt. The stems are apt to be tough, so save them for the soup, or chop and cream like celery or chard stalks. Steam the leaves until they are tender (it doesn't take long at all), boil down the juice and add butter and salt and freshly ground black pepper. That's all there is to it.

Beets can stand a little frost, but it is a good idea to get them harvested before a hard freeze. Some people claim they get "woody" if left in the ground too long, but I leave them in the garden up to the end of the season and have no complaints with the results. This may be related to the climate up here—we have cool nights. So keep an eye on your beets toward the end of the season, unless, of course, you've eaten them all up (which is not hard to do).

CHARD: I am a firm advocate of chard in home gardens. Chard substitutes nicely in my garden for spinach and celery both . . . it is slightly tougher than spinach, but five minutes extra cooking solves that problem. It is a beautiful looking plant, with a pleasant, mild taste. I use it for cooked greens and salad. It is both cool- and hot-weather hardy, doesn't go to seed readily, so it keeps producing the whole gardening season. The seeds look just like beet seeds . . . nobbly seed clusters. Plant them just like beets, thin them whenever they look crowded (into the salad first, later as cooked greens). When the plants stop crowding each other, cut the largest leaves from the plants as you need them. (By the way, chard doesn't cook down as much as spinach does, so you don't have to cut as much.) Chard makes thick stalks. I chop these stalks into the salad like celery, with excellent results. I also cream them like celery.

There are a number of kinds of chard. I grow three of them. Swiss chard has dark green leaves with a pale green stem. Red chard has bright red stalks with bright green leaves, truly a magnificent-looking plant. The third is rhubarb chard—dark red stalks with deep purple leaves. I plant them alternately in the same row: a foot of Swiss chard, a foot of red chard, a foot of rhubarb chard. The effect is glorious. Visitors' eyes light up when they see it. I've been converting everyone I know to growing chard, and one taste usually does all the convincing necessary. Try some! As a bonus it freezes beautifully, cans well, and, as I say, one planting produces crop after crop all season long.

CARROTS: Carrots are really very easy to grow, *if* you have loosened the ground sufficiently before preparing the seed bed. Just consider it for a moment: the part of the carrot plant that you want most to eat is the part that grows underground. If there is a large stone in the way you won't get a straight carrot. If the ground is very hard, the carrot has to spend a lot of energy pushing a place for itself in that hard packed ground. Result: a puny carrot. If the ground is loose, and fairly well gone over for rocks, parts of tires, old tools, etc. (all of which are normal occurrences in every American garden I've ever heard of), then the carrot has room to make a nice succulent root. *That is, if the row is thinned!* But I'm getting ahead of my story.

Carrot seed is manageable in size. I draw a line in the soil, sprinkle in some composted manure, then place the seeds one by one about a pencil width apart. Since carrots take a while to poke their greens up above the soil, I plant a radish seed every inch or so along the row. The radishes come up quickly, so I can see where the row is. They also mature quickly, so that by the time the carrots need the room, the radishes have all been eaten. This is called companion planting.

Carrots have tops that look like finely cut parsley. As soon as you can tell the plants apart, thin them. After a few weeks, these have lengthened out and a new set of leaves appear from out of the crown of the carrot. That's when I start pulling carrots for use. At this stage they are tiny, about the thickness of a pencil. I thin these carrots right into the salad. From this time on, I continue pulling carrots whenever they get to looking crowded, or when I want some to eat. If your initial seeding has been too heavy you will have to thin before the carrots reach an edible stage. Thin them out enough so you can see that no carrots are coming out of the same hole. When you've got it down that far, let them grow a bit and start thinning for table use, as before.

Carrots need occasional cultivation. A couple of times a month, I weed them thoroughly and loosen up the soil between the rows with a hoe or a cultivator. This keeps the earth loose enough so they can grow.

By the way, when I pull a carrot I try to remember to tuck the soil back around its neighbors. If the top of the carrot roots grows in sunlight, it will turn green and bitter where exposed. So I find it pays to "hill up" once along the row (whack dirt over them with a hoe).

To harvest carrots, pull them. Grab the top close to the ground and pull up with a steady pressure (I find that too fast a jerk breaks off the top, leaving the carrot behind). If the ground is packed down or very dry they may not come out easily. If you only want a few, take an old table fork out to the garden with you and push it into the ground next to the carrot you're after, and grabbing both fork handle and carrot greens, pull up. If you are harvesting a whole lot of them, use a garden fork. Shove it down into the soil as deep as you can on one side of the row, wiggle it a bit, pull it out and do the same on the other side of the row . . . then pry up with the fork until a clump of carrots is loosened up, then pull them. Some of them might break, but I find it works pretty well.

By the way, a friend told me to use the carrot greens in soups. Not very surprisingly, they taste like carrots. I also dry some chopped carrot greens for winter soups and garnishes.

Carrots don't make seed until the second year, so if you want carrot seed for your pickling spice mixture, just plant a couple of ready grown carrots and let them go. Or, easier yet, find some wild carrots growing in your back field . . . the common name for them is Queen Anne's lace. When the flower closes and the seeds are obviously brown and dry, brush them off, spread them out to dry a little longer, and pack them away.

Carrots can stand one hard freeze. More than one won't kill them, but might make for a poorer texture.

Carrots can, freeze, and store fresh in the root cellar.

The Summer Garden

When all chance of frost has passed, I plant the following heavy producers. These are our summer staples, and provide much of our winter canned and frozen food as well:

BEANS: There are all sorts of beans—soy beans, lima beans, navy beans—but the only types I've grown so far are green string beans, yellow "wax" beans, and the Italian flat green beans.

All beans are very frost sensitive, so they can't be planted until all danger of frost has gone by. I draw a line in the soil, sprinkle manure along the line, then poke holes an inch apart and drop in the beans. Then I cover them with dirt and pat them down firmly. Usually just a few days later the little bean plants have started coming up.

There are "bush" varieties and "pole" varieties of beans. As one might guess the pole ones are climbers, so to grow them you have to put something they can run up. The most traditional things are poles. We grew some pole beans this year, so Mel went out back and cut down some saplings. He sharpened the tops with his hatchet and drove them in along the row, a couple of feet apart. I drew my lines in circles around the poles, and proceeded as before.

Beans *really* must be thinned to produce well. Follow
the directions on the seed package about spacing.

The plants first make two rather heart-shaped leaves.
Then out from between these another set of leaves appears.
The beans begin to bush out (or if it is a climbing variety, to
make tendrils and climb). I try to keep the beans weeded
until they get to a pretty good size, at which point they do
much of their own weeding, shading out competitors.

One day the bean plants begin making white flowers. At
this point I look at the plants *daily* because very soon
thereafter I have beans, and from then on I have to pick over
the row every two or three days (depending on the weather
. . . less frequently during a dry spell). The idea is to catch the
beans before they toughen up, but when the pods have just
"fleshed out."

Although there are bugs that specialize in eating bean
plants, I haven't any to speak of. One day this summer I
discovered why. I was in another part of the garden, but
spied a bug on a bean plant. I hopped over very quickly, and
began to go for the bug. Then I noticed an enormous string
bean. Truly gigantic for a string bean. More like a lima bean.
Then I realized it wasn't a bean at all, it was a beautiful light
green snake—slithering along just under the top layer of
leaves from plant to plant. I watched the snake quite happily
eat the bug, so I went off to weed elsewhere and let him
continue bug-picking for me. I am personally not over-fond
of snakes, but they don't scare the daylights out of me either.
I appreciated their help. By the way, I've never seen one
while picking; I suppose they hear (or feel) me coming down
the row and get out of the way.

I found my pole beans guarded by another gardeners'
friend. A colony of large black and canary yellow spiders
built webs between the poles. They are gorgeous looking
creatures, once one gets over the initial shock of their size.
These "ladder backs" are quite harmless, I am told by gar-

dening neighbors. I made sure not to discourage their presence in the garden. As I say, I don't have bug problems, and don't want any.

If you want to avoid disease problems with beans, *never* in any way handle the plants while they are wet. Don't thin them, pick, weed them . . . don't anything them while they are wet. They are highly susceptible to damage when wet.

After a rather long peak season, the bean plants begin tapering down on their production. Toward the end, you might want to let some of them go: let the beans mature on the plant for your winter supply of "shell" (dried) beans for baked beans, soups, chili and so on. See the chapter on drying for more details.

By the way, peanuts are a form of bush beans, believe it or not. They are grown exactly like string beans are. But after they have flowered, the flowers lean over and dig themselves into the ground. The bean forms and matures underground. When the plant dies down or when there is danger of frost, pull the plants and the peanuts will come up. Because of this practice of digging themselves in, one must be sure and keep the ground nice and loose between the rows.

I saw a beautiful idea for growing pole beans in a resort town farther upstate. A gardener without much space had run strings up the sunny side of his or her garage, and had trained the pole beans up the strings. It was a pretty sight, and made for lots of beans (the vines were loaded!). If you do plant next to a building, however, choose the side that gets the most sun; and use *lots* of composted manure when planting . . . the ground right around foundations is notoriously poor.

TOMATOES: My growing season is too short to start tomatoes from seed in the garden and expect vine-ripened tomatoes before frost. So I plant tomato sets (young plants) in the garden.

The young plants come in "flats," shallow containers

with drainage holes in the bottom. There are about twelve plants to a flat. I buy them ahead of time and keep them well watered indoors for a while, and, when all danger of frost has vanished, I begin "hardening" the young plants by taking them outdoors, at first for only an hour or so during the sunniest portion of the day, working up to leaving them out all day long. This lets them gradually get accustomed to roughing it outdoors. By the end of a week they are ready to face the shock of transplanting.

I try to do all my transplanting toward dusk, but a cloudy day is also all right. Don't transplant during a hot, sunny day or the plants will suffer. Doing it late in the day gives them all night to recover before they have to face the hot sun.

Half an hour or so before I'm going to set them out, I give them a good soaking (until the earth in the flat is almost muddy). Then I go off and dig all the holes I'll need (two whacks with the grub hook, then I loosen the dirt at the bottom of the hole with the pickax end of the grub hook so the roots will be able to travel). I put a trowelful or more composted manure in each hole, and I'm ready for the plants.

I get out a flat of tomato plants, break it so I can get at a corner, and carefully break off a hunk of dirt containing one plant. The fine roots that have traveled into adjoining parts of the flat just pull out of the very wet dirt, rather than getting broken off. I put the plant in one of the holes I've dug, a little bit deeper than it sat in the flat. (Along the stem there are little white bumps which look like maggots. These are infant roots. I put the plant in deep enough so that these are underground. This ensures a good root structure for the plant). I put back the soil and press it down as firmly as I can with my hands, really leaning into it. Then I water the plant and the area immediately around the plant very thoroughly. That's all there is to it.

Aftercare of transplants: For a couple of weeks after the

plant has been set out, I try to make sure to water it well every day. If the weather is particularly hot, I sometimes put a bushel basket or a cardboard box over the newly set out plant for two or three days. You have to expect that for a couple of days after transplanting, the newly set out plant will look wilty and droopy during the hottest portion of the day. This will soon pass, though, as long as it is kept watered.

While the plants are still young, I try to keep them well weeded, and once every week or two I loosen up the soil around them with a hoe. After a while the plants will get big enough to shade out most weeds, so a little extra care in the beginning doesn't seem excessive.

The only other care they require is when the plants are at the point that they are about to flop over, I hill up around them; that is, I whack extra dirt around their bases. This is useful since it makes the plants less vulnerable to wind damage, and it lets the stem keep on making extra roots.

Tomato plants are vines. If left alone, they will make a number of branches which will sprawl around. A tomato plant first makes leaves and new branches (the branches grow out of the crook between the stem and the main leaves). Then it forms clusters of flower buds. These open up into small but beautiful yellow flowers. Bees buzz around for a while and eventually the flowers wither and you begin to see tiny tomatoes forming. The tomatoes grow bigger (while other branches continue making new flowers). When the tomatoes reach full size they begin to turn a sort of whitish color; this is the first sign of ripening. Then the whitish tinge begins getting sort of pink, and the tomato ripens up.

There are a number of styles of growing tomatoes. Some people (including me) like to let the tomato plants do what they want. I got lots of tomatoes this way, but they don't ripen up very quickly; so I modified my approach this past summer. I waited until the vines had lots of tomatoes, and I began pruning. I took off all the big leaves, which keep the sun from getting at the tomatoes. I left on the little leaves at the end of the branches, however, because I wanted to let the vines keep making new flowers. Toward the end of the season, I started cutting off the little branches which wouldn't amount to anything, as Mel's father puts it.

Some people stake their tomatoes up so the tomatoes will be off the ground. I've tried staking them up, but I can't manage it. I'm too timid.

Anyone who ever made tomato sauce starting with fresh tomatoes will know that tomatoes are mostly water. If a dry spell comes along, the tomatoes won't do much growing. If the dry spell lasts a couple of weeks, and then a soaking rain comes all at once, the tomatoes will start growing like mad, and they will "weather crack." The skin won't grow as fast as the tomato does, and so it cracks, usually in circular cracks around the stem end of the tomato. This is relatively harmless, although usually instructions for canning whole tomatoes by the cold-pack method specify that the tomatoes should not be weather cracked. My garden stays pretty moist even during dry spells, because we almost invariably have a heavy dewfall at night (there were only two occasions last summer when there was no dewfall) so mine don't weather crack. If you aren't so fortunate about dewfall, however, you might want to try watering the plants every so often during an extended dry spell. Use your judgment about frequency (look at the ground and see how parched it looks). Always water late in the day so the plants get the water, not the surrounding air. Of course, if the plants begin getting yellow and droopy from lack of water, weed thoroughly and water them as best you can.

I've grown beefsteak tomatoes and Italian plum tomatoes because I like them. Actually, these have a long growing season, so next year I'll try some of the shorter-seasoned ones. Check your seed catalogs. There are hundreds of varieties of tomatoes: giant ones, dwarf ones, early ones, late ones, red, orange and yellow ones. You'll just have to sniff around until you find out what you like, and what's likely to give you the best harvest in your locality.

If you do let your tomatoes sprawl around, you might have problems with the tomatoes that touch the ground being insect damaged or rotting. We solve this by slipping cardboard under the vines when the tomatoes are about to turn.

The only bug problems I've had with tomatoes so far occurred early in the plants' life, when we got some tiny black leaf hoppers that chew holes in the leaves. I got all panicky when they showed up, and my tomato leaves started getting lacy. I looked them up in a bug book, however, and found that their season was so very short they wouldn't permanently damage any but very sickly plants. I picked a few off to make me feel better, then forgot about them. Sure enough, after a couple of weeks, the leaf hoppers disappeared and the tomatoes were growing as well as they ever had. Later in the season a few slugs ate into the ripening tomatoes. Slugs are snails without shells, slimy creatures that can't stand hot sun, so I pick them off at dusk and feed them to the chickens. There are other bugs that attack tomatoes, but I haven't had any experience with them so I can't say much about them. I make a practice, however, of looking at the underside of the leaves for anything resembling egg cases. When I find anything at all suspicious-looking, I pick off that leaf and burn it.

If you have any sickly looking plants, pull them out and burn them immediately. Sometimes a nursery will pass along a really nasty fungus.

PEPPERS: When I planted my first garden and decided to put in some sweet peppers, I asked the woman at the nursery how many plants she suggested I get. "It depends on the season," she said. "There are some years you get peppers, there are some years you don't." It was a year for no peppers (I only got a few tiny ones from my three plants).

Last year I started my hot pepper plants indoors for transplanting. I bought those little pots made of peat moss, filled them with a mixture of top soil and well-composted manure, poked a couple of holes in the center, dropped a pepper seed into each hole, covered the seed, and watered the pot well. After a few days little pepper plants came up. I thinned them down to the single biggest plant per pot and set them in a fairly sunny window, and watered them whenever they looked dry. So far so good.

What I should have done next when they grew to two inches high was to transplant them (pots and all) into larger peat pots, but I kept thinking the garden would be ready any day, so I left them in the little pots. They finally got set out (same procedure as transplanting tomatoes, except you plant pot and all, and rip the pot on one side when you plant, so the roots travel better). I got lots of nice big, very hot peppers, but the plants stayed quite small. Maybe they were supposed to be small, I don't really know. I've never seen any other hot pepper plants. I didn't have any bug problems. My main problem was to keep little Miriam from trying one, they looked so appealing!

A VERY IMPORTANT WARNING: Whenever you handle hot peppers, fresh or dry, be *sure* and wash your hands before you touch your eyes. If you do get some in your eye, it will sting like the dickens. Flush the eye with plenty of cold water until it stops stinging.

SQUASH, CUCUMBERS, MELONS, PUMPKINS: These are all slightly different versions of the same plant. All are frost sensitive. And if you plant more than one of them, be *sure* to separate them widely, because they cross. Your melons will taste like squash. *You are warned!*

I don't have a long enough season to grow melons . . . I tried the first year, but didn't get anywhere. As far as pumpkins are concerned, I like them well enough, but find winter squash more versatile, so I grow that instead. There are *many* types and each has its own good points. I fully plan to spend the rest of my life trying out new and interesting ones. The first year, I grew acorn squash, the second year I grew blue hubbard. Next year, I plan to try that sweet, beautifully textured and gorgeously decorative Turks Turban (it really looks like its name!).

Some squash varieties are vines, others are bushes. Until recently the rule seemed to be that many summer squash were bush style, and the winter squash were vine style. Recently, however, some of the seed companies have been breeding bush-type winter squash for gardeners who don't have enormous space . . . and believe me, squash vines can get enormous. Blue hubbard requires ten square feet per hill! Some people solve the space problem by companion planting. They plant pumpkins (they also make vines) or winter squash in their corn patch. By the time the vine starts "running," a couple of cultivations have given the corn all the start it needs, so they don't interfere with each other. Indeed, since the vine squashes have enormous leaves, they help shade out the weeds in the corn patch. The only difficulty I've encountered with squash in the corn patch is that come some catastrophe which flattens the corn (and I've had one each year), the squash will grab on to the corn with its tendrils and keep it from "coming back," that is, from pulling itself upright.

Some people solve the space problem by planting vine squash (or cucumbers, or melons) at the edge of the garden and training it out into the lawn.

Squash (bush or vine), cucumbers, melons, pumpkins, I plant in "hills." That is, I remove a trowelful or so of soil, add as much composted manure, poke a hole and drop in five to ten seeds, depending on what I'm planting (see the instructions). I pat down the dirt over the seeds, and after a while a whole bunch of little plants come up. Then I pull all but two or three of the strongest plants (this is *highly* necessary thinning! If you don't thin now, you won't get any fruit at all, as one friend of mine found out . . . even if the vines look healthy!). I weed around the "hill" until the remaining plants can take care of themselves. Once the plants really start growing they do most of their own weeding by shading out new growth.

Then one glorious day the plants develop two kinds of flashy yellow blossoms; one kind will make fruit, the other won't. You can tell the difference by looking at the flower stems. If it is a zucchini plant, the flowers with skinny, pale green stems won't make zucchinis. But the flowers with tiny zucchinis for stems will fruit. The flowers open and close daily for a few days, bees buzz around, and one day the flower closes for good, and the zucchini starts growing. When this happens, I knock the blossom off the stem of the zucchini. If I don't, sometimes the blossom starts rotting and the rot spreads to the zucchini. I've never had a squash begin to rot on the vine if I've removed the closed blossom! If one does begin to rot, pick it, cut out the rotten part and use the good parts at once. Don't can it, though, for it won't keep.

If you are growing summer squash, be sure and pick the fruit while it is immature. The smaller you pick it the better it tastes. *Don't* let it get enormous, because the skin toughens up and the seeds get big and hard. When the plant starts bearing, look it over every day, especially in moist weather. Zucchinis can bulb out overnight! And by the way, the more you pick the more you get. I know this for a fact, because this year I let one extraordinarily healthy zucchini ripen up for winter storage, but the plant did not produce as *many* zucchinis as my others. It stands to reason, since the plant had to feed my big zucchini rather than start new shoots.

The first year, I grew zucchini (summer squash) and acorn squash (for winter squash). This year, I planted zucchini again, and yellow squash (also a summer squash), and something variously called St. Patricks Squash, Patty Pan, scalloped squash or Flying Saucer Squash (the flat white scalloped squashes look like flying saucers ought to look). I love them all dearly and will certainly plant all three again.

To pick summer squash I make a small slit in the stem with a small paring knife, then twist the squash off the plant. Twisting it without the slit doesn't work too well, because the squash tends to break off without a stem. Winter squash should be left on the vine as long as possible, but not be allowed to freeze. Squash that has turned color and hardened up can stand a light frost. But if it hasn't started turning, it will get frost damage. When there is a danger of frost, I pick off all the immature winter squash and bring them inside. I serve them like summer squash, work them into a chutney, or if they have begun to turn at all, I put them in a window to ripen up. If cold weather hits, I bring in all the winter squash and store it in a cool place. Those not quite "ready" will ripen up nicely indoors. Leave a bit of stem on for storage.

Speaking of harvesting, the first time I reached down to pick a cucumber I jumped back in fright. I was sure something had bitten me. The damn things are prickly! The prickles scrub off with a vegetable brush.

CORN: Corn is really easy to grow, but *must* be planted when the soil is ready, or it just won't germinate. Ready means that excess water has drained out, and there is no danger of a freeze. The seed, obviously, is a corn kernel.

There are two styles of growing corn: in hills or in rows. Either way it is not necessary to prepare a fine seed bed. We plant in ground which has been plowed only. (It does help to rake out weed roots, however.) I plant corn in hills. I make a hole with a dibble (a dibble is a piece of sharpened broomstick stuck into a handle), sprinkle in a handful or so of composted manure, and drop five or six kernels into it, cover them, and pat them down firmly. Since we cultivate the corn patch using a rototiller, we make sure the "hills" are far enough apart to let the rototiller through. After a week or so, if conditions are right, the corn comes up. Corn is a grass, believe it or not, and the young corn plants look just like grass, so that the first weeding can be a little bit of a nuisance. But luckily, the young corn blades are somewhat thicker and slightly brighter green than the grass that grows around here, so it is not too much of a hassle. What we do is this. As soon as the corn is up, I go through the patch finding the hills and hoeing around each hill of corn. I also thin them, leaving three or four of the strongest corn plants to each hill. Now Mel can rototill.

We cultivate once or twice more before the corn gets knee high and it gets hard to go through with the rototiller. After this last cultivation I "hill up" around the corn (whack dirt around the stalks) so wind won't knock the plants over. Corn has a very shallow root system and will fall down if you look at it. Then I broadcast-sow turnips in the corn patch if I haven't planted any squash. To broadcast-sow any kind of seed, mix it well in half a bucket of fine dirt, and toss the mixture around. I tried broadcasting without mixing and my planting was much too thick.

One fine day the corn begins making tassels. They come out of the top of the plant, have little seed-like gadgets on them, and make lots of pollen. The wind blows the pollen around, some of it settles where the leaves come out of the stems, and soon the little ears of corn begin to form there. (Because corn is dependent on wind for fertilization, it is better to plant corn in a block rather than in a single long row. That way some of the plants are always downwind.) When the ears get bigger, the silk sticking out of the ears begins to turn brown and dry up, and when it is good and dry, and you can feel the corn kernels have "fleshed out," it is ready to eat.

If left on the stalks too long the kernels get starchy, so to spread out the corn season many people either space their plantings (start them a couple of weeks apart), or plant two varieties: an early and later variety.

This year, we had very heavy rain in July with attendant flash flooding down the mountain. My corn patch was under water for a week or so. I dug ditches to drain off the water, and since standing water leeches nitrogen out of the soil, I decided to fertilize it when the water went down. I half filled a bucket with chicken manure, added a lot of water and walked down the row with the hose running into the bucket. Liquid manure spilled out between the rows (but *not* on the plants—it would burn them). Within a couple of days the corn started growing like mad. (I have found out that liquid fresh chicken manure is death on squash, and turnips don't like it either.)

One day when I was in the corn patch, I noticed that the husk of one ear of corn had broken open, and enormous black things that looked like tree fungus were growing out of the kernels. Mel's father told me it was corn smut, and to pick the ear off right away and burn or bury it.

That's all I can say about corn, except that it is impossible for a city dweller to obtain real sweet corn. When corn comes in season we have a ritual. Fifteen minutes before dinner Mel goes out into the corn patch. Meanwhile I set a kettle to boil. He picks enough sweet corn for a meal, husks it, takes off the silk, the corn goes right into the pot, and we eat it as a separate course. Nothing, but nothing, not even porterhouse steak, should interfere with sweet corn. It is a mystical experience.

Corn may be frozen, canned, or may be dried on the cob when mature for corn meal. Corn is frost sensitive, so plan your harvest accordingly.

POTATOES: Last year was the first time I grew potatoes. They were not a raving success by any means, but that was our fault. We were growing them in sod that had been plowed under, but not removed. So far so good. We had planned to plant the potatoes far enough apart so we could cultivate with the rototiller, but they turned out to be not only too close, but actually wavy. It was then that we realized it was not enough to measure the width of the rototiller when planning row widths. It is necessary to add space for the actual plants. It is also not advisable to step on the garden line when digging the holes.

We did get about sixty pounds of potatoes from our patch. We grew our potatoes by buying so-called "seed" potatoes at the local Agway. We cut them into pieces and planted those. We discovered, after the fact, that it is advisable to store the seed potatoes in a warm place for a few days before cutting them so they can sprout a bit. Then it is easy to see where the "eyes" are. The potatoes should be cut in such a way that each piece has an eye or two. If you want big potatoes, the potato piece should have only one eye. If you want lots of smaller potatoes, the pieces can have more than one eye. Each eye will make a potato plant. Mel's father tells me that it is advisable to cut seed potatoes lengthwise. He showed me that with a careful search it is possible to find where the potato had been attached to the plant . . . it is a sort of dried up stem-like appendage on each potato. Cut from that to the opposite side. Little potatoes should be left whole. Big ones can be cut into four or five pieces, depending on the number of eyes and the size of the potato. If there are too many eyes on a piece of potato, some may be cut out and discarded. The potato pieces should be allowed to dry out in air for a day or two after cutting and before planting, so they can scar the cut over and become less susceptible to rot. It takes about two weeks for potatoes to send up vines. The young shoots are a dark green.

When we were ready to plant, we set up a garden line. Three of us were working. Mel dug the holes (about four inches deep). I dropped the potato piece in, stepped on it (this sent it an inch or so deeper) and piled the dirt back over the potato (*don't* add manure—it makes for scabby potatoes). Mel's father went behind us and tamped down the dirt with a hoe. It didn't take long at all.

Due to my inexperienced cutting, there were occasional gaps in the row. When the plants were up and we discovered we couldn't get through with a rototiller, we had to weed by hand. The little cultivator didn't make a dent in the soddy grassy ground. So Mel and I went out with a grubhook and hoe and whacked away. We did manage to keep the upper end of the potato patch somewhat weeded throughout the season, but the lower end did pretty much as it wanted. Result: the plants were weaker and less productive at the weedy end. When the plants get bushy, they begin to flower. Potato flowers are beautiful; they look like tomato flowers, except that they are white and pale purple. Very delicate looking. Mel's father showed me how to look at the underside of the leaves for egg clusters.

After a time, the plants stop flowering and just sit there. At this point it is well to hill up around the plant, whack dirt around its base with a hoe, so any potatoes the plant decides to make near the surface won't turn green in the sunlight. ALL GREEN PARTS OF POTATO PLANTS (INCLUDING THE SPROUTS AND FRUITS) ARE POISONOUS! Some time later, the vines begin to get brown and wither away. Once they are entirely withered the potatoes have grown their fullest and are ready for digging.

You dig potatoes with something called a potato fork. It is like a garden fork, except bent at the neck. Mel figured out how to use it. You look for the hill of potatoes, give a good swing with the potato fork, hitting about half an inch from the hill, and pull up. Once you've got the hang of it, you will pull up the whole potato plant with the potatoes attached. Before you get the hang of it you will spear the potatoes, which is a nuisance that only practice does away with. Use the speared potatoes first, because they won't keep as long.

Along with the big potatoes and the medium-sized potatoes, there will be a whole batch of very tiny potatoes. Don't forget to pick these up when you harvest! They are the *best* tasting treats! Whenever I make a pot roast or a stew I use these tiny treats, skin and all. New potatoes are very tasty indeed, so try to grow at least a couple of hills to get an idea of the true potential of this food. Stored potatoes are quite different from fresh dug ones.

By all means get your potatoes in before a hard freeze. Frozen potatoes are unpalatable.

Potatoes may be stored fresh in the root cellar, or canned.

Of course you can keep your own potatoes from year to year to use for seed. But as far as garden hygiene is concerned, it is probably well to buy seed potatoes for planting every two or three years. They are heartier and the soil is less apt to develop and retain diseases specific to your strain of potatoes.

The Fall Garden

When all the summer stuff is in, I turn my attention to planning for the fall. I make additional plantings of beets, carrots, and put in a row of parsnips. This year I tried some salsify, also called oyster plant. It is a winter-hardy root plant like parsnips. Parsnips and salsify are treated just like carrots are. Since they take a long time to germinate, mark the rows with radishes.

I also put in some winter salads, escarole primarily. You grow it like lettuce, but keep it thinned from the start. It can stand some cold weather but not a great deal. It tends to be bitter, so a week before using either tie up the leaves loosely so the heart "blanches" or bleaches, which eliminates the bitterness, or cut the plant and put it in a plastic bag in a cool dark place. The first year I grew chinese cabbage for late fall salads, and was very pleased with it. It can stand some cold weather, but if it freezes it gets stringy, so avoid that. Thinnings may be used in salads, may be cooked or dried for winter soups. Mature plants may be stored for a time in the root cellar. Plant and cultivate like you do lettuce or chard. Cut mature plants to harvest.

The second year I couldn't get any chinese cabbage seed for some reason, so I planted Florentine fennel instead. This tastes like licorice. Plant and cultivate like lettuce, keep it thinned (into the salad), and cut when the bottom stalk bulbs out, but before it begins to lengthen (they do this when they go to seed). I steep the finely cut tops in vinegar for a tarragon-like vinegar; and cut the stalks into salads. They store for a short time in the root cellar.

For late fall menus, I rely mostly on members of the cabbage family. They are all cool-weather hardy, and so provide up to two extra months of garden fresh vegetables. All sorts of unexpected things are members of this family; the line up includes broccoli, kale, Brussels sprouts, cauliflower, cabbage, kohlrabi, and collards. Anything with "brassica" in its botanical name comes into this category. A little more distantly related are radishes and turnips. Because all these things are related, they tend to have the same pests and to

be afflicted with the same sorts of diseases, so they should not
be planted in the same area in successive years. If you keep
them together, planning next year's garden will be less of a
jigsaw puzzle!

CABBAGE: There are early cabbages and late cabbages.
Many new gardeners don't know this. One neighbor of mine
planted cabbage sets early in the spring and got a fine crop
of ripe cabbage in the middle of July, just when she didn't
need cabbage. Early cabbage is not particularly good for
sauerkraut, and no basement around here is cool enough in
August to store cabbages. My taste is to have them maturing
just when cool weather sets in. Ask gardening folk in your
area for a decent timetable on cabbage.

Cabbage first makes two leaves, then makes a second set
of leaves, and after that gradually forms a loose head. As the
season goes on, the head begins to firm up. If it grows too
much, the head will begin to split. This is when you must cut
it. If all your cabbages are maturing at once, grab by the base
the plants you don't want to use immediately and "lift" up
a little. The idea is to pull it hard enough to break some of
the little roots, but not hard enough to pull it out of the
ground. This will slow down the plant's growth somewhat, so
it won't burst before you get a chance to eat it. A veteran
gardener told me that trick. It works.

Cabbage plants don't require much care once they get
started. But until they are well established, it is a good idea
to hoe around the plants every few days for a couple of weeks
to keep the soil loose, so the roots can travel. With a thorough
weeding once every three or four weeks for the rest of the
season the plants will take care of themselves. Same goes for
Brussels sprouts, cauliflower, kale and brocoli.

KALE: Home grown kale is very different from the city
version. First of all it is not sour . . . but I suspect organic
gardening does that. It is hearty, tender and actually sweet.
It can be used as it grows. I seed it right in the row, thin

young plants into the salad, and as they develop large leaves I break them off for cooking, leaving the little ones to develop. Kale is at its best tastewise after a freeze.

I freeze it, and dry some of the thinnings for winter soups.

Kale, like all members of the cabbage family, wants to be well fertilized. So if you are not transplanting but seeding in the row, spread composted manure thickly along the row before you fork it over. The forking will mix the composted manure in with the soil very well; then follow the procedure for planting small seed.

BRUSSELS SPROUTS: A neighbor of mine and I split a flat of Brussels sprouts this past summer. I didn't use any of mine until after the frost (frost improves the flavor of this vegetable too). She was disappointed in her sprouts, and I was surprised because mine were sweet and lovely and mild. Then I found out she wasn't peeling them. The outer leaves of sprouts are bitter from the sun so they should be removed before cooking. I also started some sprouts in the garden, and they produced just as well as the sets did, but later in the season, which was fine with me, since I use them as a fall vegetable. The top of the Brussels sprout plant looks like a cabbage plant. The sprouts grow out from the nook between the main stem and each leaf, so this is where to watch for the sprouts, not on top of the plant. Every plant has lots of sprouts maturing at different times, so it is handy to have a few plants going.

When the Brussels sprouts are nice and firm, snap them off the stem by pressing down with your thumb. As the Brussels sprouts grow big they cut off circulation in the leaf just below, and that leaf begins to yellow. Feel free to knock it off the plant and to give the sprout more room to grow.

Brussels sprouts store fresh in the root cellar for a short time, freeze beautifully, and may be canned.

CAULIFLOWER: I haven't had any luck with cauliflower. I planted it the first year, and while the plants grew to an enormous size, they never got around to flowering. It might have had something to do with the fact that during the very wet spring they were under water for about two weeks. I didn't try any this past year, but a neighbor of mind did, and she got plenty of cauliflower. A week before she wants to use a cauliflower, she loosely ties up the large leaves so the sun can't get at the head. This "bleaches" the head so it is pretty and white. Cauliflower freezes well, and may be stored for a short time in a root cellar.

BROCCOLI: I started broccoli plants indoors this year and transplanted them to the garden. Next year I will set them in late, since I don't use broccoli until fall, and it must be picked when it is ready or else it bursts into flower and makes seeds. It is mature when there is a large broccoli cluster in the center of the plant; cut it when the buds are just beginning to loosen up a little. Then, the main flower gone, the plant will make branches each with a new, but smaller, broccoli. Cut these, too, as they are ready for use. As usual, fertilize heavily when planting.

TURNIPS: Even people who don't like turnips might just find that garden fresh, organically grown turnips pulled right after a frost are sweet enough for their tastes. That veteran gardener I keep talking about advised me to plant turnips wherever something has finished up for the season . . . lettuce, early potatoes or whatever. They may also be broadcast-sowed in the potato patch or the corn patch in midsummer for a late fall harvest. They don't like "hot" manure (uncomposted, that is). Turnips store beautifully in the root cellar and freeze well. They can also stand a good outdoor freeze. After one freeze I pull the big turnips and leave the little ones. The big turnips get stored away in the root cellar, and well into December, whenever a thaw comes around, I go out to the garden and pull the little ones for use.

If they are pulled frozen they rot, but pulled when completely thawed they are beautiful.

WINTER RADISHES: Those sharp, long white radishes
you occasionally get in the city are winter radishes. I broadcast-sowed some in next year's spring garden and got enormous quantities. They are extremely hot, but a few frosts
temper them nicely. They may be seeded in rows whenever
anything else is finished up for the season. The radishes store
well in the root cellar, and keep in mind that chickens love
the tops.

Members of the cabbage family, turnips, and radishes all
have the same enemies. One is a white butterfly which lays
pretty pea-green eggs. These grow into little caterpillars exactly the same color as a green cabbage plant. You really
have to stare at the plant awhile in order to see the eggs, on
a leaf, or where the leaf attaches to the stem. Scrape them
off. If you miss these, but start seeing holes in the leaves, stare
at the plant for a while. After a time you will begin to see the
green caterpillars . . . it's like an inkblot test. They frequently
lie in such a way as to look just like the rib on the leaf. Pick
them off and squash them, or put them in a jar and take them
far away. And if you see them on one plant, go around to all
members of the cabbage family in your garden and bug-pick.
Do this for a week and you'll have the problem solved. If you
want to be very clever, plant some purple cabbage, so just a
glance will tell you when to start searching the rest of the
family. By the way, purple cabbage stores beautifully . . . I've
had better luck storing it than green cabbage.

One home remedy that works well for these pests and
many of the other enemies of the cabbage family is to sprinkle the tops and bases of the plants with wood ash. Scatter it
while the dew is still on the leaves and it will stick nicely. It
won't make for "dirty" cabbage, since the head forms from
the inside.

By the way, if you wake up one morning and find a number of the leaves of a plant neatly cut off, think rabbits. But also think cut worms. Cut worms are a nasty garden pest. Night feeders, they climb up the stems and chew off the leaves of young plants. Scratch in the dirt around the defaced plant and see if you can find a particularly tough-looking worm with little feet. Smash him with a rock or remove him from the premises. If you can't find him, try putting a "collar" made of a milk container around the stem of the plant. This keeps the bug from being able to climb up.

Final Remark on Seed and Varieties

Even if you are not going to buy seed by mail the first year, be sure and write for some seed catalogs, and read them (not a very difficult task, let me tell you!). The catalogs have beautiful pictures, but better yet, they describe at length the features of the many varieties of each vegetable available; and give information on planting techniques, length of growing season, resistance to disease, storage qualities and so on. Reading through a couple of these catalogs will give you a feeling for the plants even if you've never seen them in the flesh. When buying seed, *do* pay attention to the estimated length of the growing season required by that variety. It is a good idea to choose varieties that mature quickly for your first garden, so you get a sense of accomplishment early in the game. And, again, if in doubt about varieties suitable for your area, check with your gardening neighbors. Home gardeners are always ready to talk about their gardens, however reserved they may be about anything else.

CHAPTER 6

CANNING

Greer speaking

I find preserving food for winter a particularly pleasurable aspect of gardening. It makes me feel secure to know that each fall, come what may, I can feed our family and an unlimited series of house guests if necessary, all through the winter. Yes, I tend to overstock, I'm like that; but it all gets used after all . . . if not by us, then by the neighbors, or, for that matter, by the chickens.

Actually, preserving food becomes a thing in itself as the season progresses. I don't have my orchard set out yet, for instance, so my in-laws and I make a project of going to pick-your-own places and stocking up on goodies like cherries, plum, peaches, pears, and apples. I watch local papers for ads telling of such places and only pick from healthy-looking plants. You don't want to spread disease to your own land! One farm I went to consisted of a field of absolutely withered tomato vines, although the tomatoes looked all right. Mel's father told me it was a fungus that hit that field. The tomatoes may have looked all right, but they were carriers of the disease!

I also comb the wild fields, when the proper time comes, for raspberries, blackberries, elderberries, wild pears and other goodies for winemaking, canning, jellies, jams, chutneys and juices. The last thing in the fall I buy wholesale, through a local farm, whatever I'll need for winter that my garden hasn't produced—a crate of cabbage, a sack or two of potatoes and onions; a sack of wheat for grinding into whole-grain flour for bread. I also visit my wholesale butcher and stock the freezer with meats, and when everything is stowed away in one form or another, I am content to get fat during the "lean months" ahead, knowing that come spring, I'll work it all off preparing for the next season of food stowing. And since each year brings plans for an expansion of our home production capacities, each year I have to buy less to get us through the winter.

In the last few years, with the aid of Mel's parents, I've learned a number of methods of food storage. Each has its advantages and disadvantages; all are useful. Food can be dried, brined, pickled, preserved, frozen raw or cooked, canned, and, in some cases, stored fresh in a root cellar. There are foods that are easy to dry because they require little preparation for the drying process (herbs, elderberries, hot peppers, mushrooms, to name a few). Others are more demanding. Apples, for instance, must be peeled and sliced before drying. Apples not only store well fresh, given proper handling and packing, but also can beautifully. Frozen vegetables are frequently thought to be superior in taste to canned ones; at least the tastes involved are closer to that of fresh-from-the garden produce. But it is worth pointing out that canned vegetables have their own tastes, and these can add pleasant variety to a winter diet. Canned peas, for example, have a particularly comforting texture and taste. Some foods can up better than they freeze—home canned tomatoes are delicious, and blueberries, which toughen when frozen, remain tender when processed by the syrupless canning method. Canned goods are easy to store, convenient to use, but require much processing time. Freezer space is always at a premium, but processing time is at a minimum. Pickling and brining frequently require small bits of attention spread out over days, but bring a whole host of not-to-be-missed tastes to the table. Jellies and condiments such as chutneys and pickles give an aura of opulence to the plainest of dinners.

We will devote a section to each method of putting food by, and will give a variety of sample recipes we feel best illustrate the techniques involved. You will decide what method to use on a particular food by taking into account how long you wish to store it, how much time you want to spend processing it, how much storage space you have, what materials you have on hand, and, of course, the taste and texture of the finished product.

Even if you live in the suburbs or the city, you can do some of these things. A surprising amount will fit under a good-sized bed! And, for that matter, even if you're not up to digging a sub-basement for a root cellar in a suburban home, a second refrigerator in the basement, or a walled off, insulated section of garage, or an unheated attic can frequently be fitted up as a root cellar. Or a barrel may be sunk under the lawn somewhere and covered with straw. There are all sorts of possibilities . . . how about lining the back of a closet with shallow shelves for storing homemade pickles, jams and conserves?

Until the era of disposable bottles of Enfamil, Similac and the other prepared baby formulas, every mother who did not breast feed did some canning . . . whether she knew it or not. The procedure she followed in preparing, bottling and sterilizing the formula for her baby was exactly the same as canning.

She mixed the formula, cleaned the bottles thoroughly, packed the formula into them, put on a disk lid and then a separate screw band, put the bottle into a "sterilizer" or kettle of boiling water and boiled them for an appropriate length of time.

Why did she go through all this? So the formula would be pure and "keep." She could mix a whole batch at once, and have it ready to use over a period of time. When she boiled the bottles of formula she was raising the milk to a high enough temperature for a long enough time to destroy the enzymes and bacteria in the milk that would cause it to spoil. (I myself never saw the point of going through all this when I was capable of producing a fresher home brew for my baby, but then each to her own.)

Canning, then, consists of giving the food some initial preparation, packing it into clean, hot jars, or cans, closing the containers and "processing" or boiling them for some time in a pot of boiling water or a pressure cooker. It requires a lot of careful attention for whole chunks of the day. It's a lot of trouble, no question about it, and if I lived in a climate where my garden produced year-round I would only do a small amount of specialty canning. But I don't live in such a climate, so during canning season (for me August through October) I harvest, "put up" food, and do little else.

Certainly a wide variety of commercially canned foods are available, so why bother? As far as we are concerned, for good reason. Commercially canned foods are expensive compared with home canned foods. But there is a better reason yet. When we do home canning we can and do prepare the food exactly to our tastes. For instance, we love canned fruit, but commercially canned fruit, with few exceptions, is slimy.

This is because it is packed in a heavy syrup. We use a light to medium syrup for canning our fruits to obtain what we feel to be a better textured and tasting product. Commercially canned beans have a "briney" taste which I dislike intensely, while by the simple expedient of leaving out the salt, we obtain a pleasant tasting canned product which can be salted later. And then there is specialty canning: pears canned with a few sprigs of fresh mint, summer savory or sage are exquisite. Minted pears are available at gourmet shops at outrageous prices, but savory or sage pears? As far as I know I invented them. (You'll find the recipe later.)

In spite of the trouble, I love canning, probably because I love to cook, and I love the results—a table lined up with row upon row of jars full of fruits and vegetables prepared exactly to taste is a pretty sight to see. And the eating can be superb! Even so, I would not recommend canning to anyone who does not thoroughly enjoy cooking. There is such a *lot* of cooking involved in canning.

How Safe Is Canning?

A year or so ago Mel introduced me to a university colleague who was in the process of a divorce. Mel, it seems, had been bragging about all the food we had put up for winter. His colleague turned to me and said, "I hear you're getting set for a good dose of botulism." Although I instantly lost a good portion of the sympathy I had felt for his marital misfortune, I said to him what I say here: the possibility of food poisoning is a point which requires the most *respectful* consideration. The safety of any canned food, whether home or commercially processed, depends on the care and precision employed by the processor. It is not that home canned food is unsafe; it is that food canned by certain canners might be unsafe. If you follow good canning procedures quite precisely, and take certain precautions when using your products, you will be in no danger of botulism or the other forms of food poisoning.

These precautions are simple enough to follow. First of all, only strictly fresh and undamaged food should be used for canning. The only exception to the former is that fruits picked slightly underripe may be ripened indoors; the only exception to the latter that I know of is in preparing canned fruit sauce, for which windfalls may be safely used if all rotten spots are discarded. All utensils used during canning should be thoroughly clean and well rinsed. And the food must be processed at high enough temperatures for a long enough time to destroy the agents of food spoilage it contains.

Botulism, for example, the most dreaded form of food poisoning, is caused indirectly by a form of bacteria called *clostridium botulinum.* Spores of this bacteria are in the soil and air some years, while they are absent other years. The bacteria are in themselves harmless, but when they develop in an *airless low-acid* environment they produce a toxin which is deadly.

Under ordinary circumstances boiling water is *never* hotter than 212°. Molds, enzymes and yeasts are destroyed when subjected to this temperature for a period of time, but the botulism bacteria are not: they require a temperature of 240°.

Since we want a temperature hotter than ordinary boiling water to take care of these bacteria, we must do something out of the ordinary, namely, increase the pressure. The higher the pressure the hotter the temperature at which water boils. The whole point of a pressure canner is not the pressure, but the temperatures it makes possible. When vegetables and meats are processed at ten pounds pressure they reach a temperature of 240°. If they are processed long enough at this temperature, they are perfectly safe.

There is a marginal chance, however, that something might have gone wrong during the canning process. Perhaps something was wrong with the pressure gauge; perhaps the processing time was improperly calculated; maybe the jar or can was defective; or some such exceptional circumstance took place. To guard against this eventuality, we make a habit of boiling all *low-acid* home canned products for at least fifteen minutes *before even tasting* them. This fifteen minutes at ordinary boiling temperature destroys any trace of botulism toxin which might be present in the canned product. (Of course if you are using the canned food in a casserole which will be baked at 350° for an hour or more, you won't have to boil the food first.)

The upshot of all this is that home canned vegetables and meats are slightly less convenient to use than their commercially canned equivalents (although cases of botulism from commercially canned soups have cropped up within the past few years and would have been avoided had the product been (1) carefully prepared, and (2) boiled fifteen minutes before use).

Canned fruits, pickles, chutneys and jams, of course do not require this ten minutes of boiling. Their high-acid content protects them against this sort of contamination: the bacteria cannot develop in a high-acid environment.

The other precaution we take is never to use any canned product that shows signs of spoilage: discoloration, bad smell, mold (except on jellies and jams; this mold is harmless though unsightly, and may be scraped off and the uncontaminated part of the product used); and we never use canned foods from containers that leak before opening, or that spurt or hiss when first opened. (Of course there will be a slight hiss when a vacuum-packed jar is first opened . . . this doesn't count.)

Which boils down to the *most important thing about canning. Never do anything that makes you nervous about the quality of the finished product when canning.* If you do you will have fantasies of botulism and all the other forms of food poisoning every time you use your home-produced article.

Materials and Utensils for Canning

I have never used tin cans for canning, so I can't say anything about the techniques involved. If you want to use them and can locate a source for getting them I suspect they come with instructions. A special (and expensive) sealing device is necessary.

I use jars for canning. I have both the old-fashioned glass-lidded jars with the attached wire clamps, now no longer made as far as I know; and the more readily available "mason jars" with the two-piece metal "dome" lids. Some people swear by one type, others say they have more luck with the other. Since the dome-lidded jars are slightly easier to use, and since the lids for them are readily available, it is probably more sensible to start collecting these.

Canning jars come in a variety of sizes, from half-pint "jelly jars" to half-gallon jars useful for pickles. I have found the pint and quart sizes most useful. There is a new size available, a one-and-a-half-pint jar, which I do not use. Since my twenty-one-quart Presto pressure canner takes a double layer of pints, but only a single layer of the pint-and-a-half jars, I would lose something on quantity. If I want something larger than pints, I use quarts.

Canning jars may be bought second hand at resale places, garage sales, and auctions. If you are buying by the jar (rather than by the box) run your finger over each jar top to make sure it is not chipped. If you are buying the glass-lidded clamp style jar, check both jar top (especially the glass ledge just under the rim) and the lid. A chipped jar won't seal and is therefore useless. I am not willing to pay more than a nickel apiece for pints, and a dime for quarts, second hand, much less than their cost new.

At second-hand stores mason jars usually lack lids, but lids are readily available. In any case, only the screw-on band part of the lid is reusable. The flat gummed disk part is not reusable. If you see the very old one-piece metal-lidded canning jars, you might want to buy them as collector's items (they're getting to be worth money these days) but don't use them. They are not considered safe.

Canning jars come in two mouth styles: wide-mouthed and regular. I used to shrug at warnings to buy only wide-mouthed jars if possible. But I've been converted. The wide-mouthed jars are much easier to pack, more food fits into the jar, and they allow awkwardly shaped foods (like whole brandied peaches) to go in without being cut up. Since I already have a large number of the regular-mouthed canning jars, I use these for liquid sorts of things, like juices, soup stock, applesauce and berries.

New jars can be purchased from Sears and in many country and countrified grocery and department stores during the summer months. If you are buying new jars, you might consider the recently available "can-or-freeze" jars. These are put out by Ball (a leading manufacturer of canning supplies), and are tempered to withstand both very high and very low temperatures. They are therefore versatile if you do freezing as well. They are wide-mouthed and are flared so it is easy to get food in and out (a necessity for frozen food) and are easy to clean.

Certain kinds of jars from store-bought foods reseal. Many baby-food jars and peanut butter jars do. I use these for pickles and jams, things that require no processing after packing. I do not trust them in the canner. Others, like many quart-size mayonnaise jars, are designed so that the regular-size mason jar dome lids fit them. (Good country housewives used to buy commercially prepared foods with an eye not only to quality and price, but to the reuse of the containers; packaging in a "mason jar" was considered quite a selling-point. Unfortunately the trend was broken and many of the larger size mayonnaise jars just miss properly fitting the wide-mouth dome lids available.) Again, I use these in a pinch, but only for things that don't go into the canner. Others of my friends and relations use instant coffee jars of the style in which Nescafé is packed, with their original lids. This makes me nervous, so I don't do it.

CANNERS: There are two types of "canners" or pots in which canning may conveniently be done. One is a hot-water bath canner, the other a pressure canner.

A *hot-water bath canner* consists of an enormous agate (or enameled) kettle with a lid and a wire rack into which seven, eight or nine canning jars fit, depending on the size of the canner. If you come across an aluminum one, don't get it: you won't be able to use it for pickling or winemaking, important secondary uses for this style of canner. Mine cost about five dollars new, so it is worthwhile getting a new one. If you get a used one, make sure the inside enamel isn't chipped. If it is chipped you can't use it for pickling.

The wire racks that come with these canners are usually designed so that once the canner is full of jars, the handles of the rack may be folded down over the top of the jars. When the canner is full of boiling water, the handles may be easily fished up with a fork. The whole canner-load of jars may then be lifted part way up and hooked onto the sides of the pot by means of a bend in the handles. This design of the rack handles is extremely convenient, because then the hot jars may be taken out one by one with no danger of scalding yourself. A rack full of full canning jars is extraordinarily heavy! I would insist on this style rack. If you do get stuck with a rack with no handles, however, leave the center space empty so you can ladle out the hot water with a soup dipper until the lids of the jars are exposed, allowing the processed jars to be lifted out without reaching into boiling water.

Fruit may be canned with perfect safety in a reasonable amount of time in a hot-water bath canner (ten minutes to half an hour, depending on the fruit). Vegetables require two to three hours for safe processing in boiling water, which I consider outrageous, and there is a distinct element of risk in canning low-acid vegetables or meats in this type of canner. The processing temperature reached by boiling water is just not high enough to kill all agents of spoilage for these products.

A *pressure canner* provides the answer here. Since I am not one of those people who have a horror of pressure cookers, I use my pressure canner for canning all vegetables and meats, and some fruits as well. Food processed in a pressure canner at five pounds pressure reaches a temperature of 228°, perfectly safe for fruits; ten pounds pressure brings the temperature to 240°, safe for vegetables and meats. The advantage in safety is enhanced by a substantial decrease in processing time: string beans, for instance, take twenty-five minutes at ten pounds pressure (a temperature of 240°) as compared with three hours in a boiling water bath (temperature 212°)!

Pressure canners are like ordinary pressure cookers except that they are enormous, and have a pressure gauge that registers the pressure inside the canner at any given moment. This is important, as noted above.

Pressure canners come in two sizes, sixteen-quart and twenty-one-quart capacity. The difference in price is not substantial, so I would recommend the twenty-one-quart size. This size has room for seven quart jars or eighteen of the pint-sized, dome-lidded mason jars. (These may be stacked.

Unfortunately, however, only one layer of the wireclamp
glass-lidded pints fits in, another good reason for using dome-
lidded mason jars if you have a choice.) My canner, a Presto,
cost about thirty-five dollars new, and is worth every cent of
it. We decided on a Presto because parts and service for this
brand are readily available. Montgomery Ward and Sears
Roebuck both carry them.

Occasionally a pressure canner will come up at an auction or garage sale. Indeed, I saw one go at a local school
auction for 50¢. If you buy one this way there are certain
things you should look for.

Make sure it has an instruction book with it. You should
never operate a pressure canner without reading *the instruction manual written for that model* canner. If it is a relatively
new one, and of a known brand, you *might* be able to obtain
one from its manufacturer.

Look at the pressure gauge. This is a clock-like dial sticking up out of the lid. It should register zero. This is extremely
important for safety's sake. If the pressure gauge is broken,
you may build up dangerous levels of pressure in the canner
without knowing it. Or you might use too little pressure and
cause your food to spoil. You also would not be able to tell
when the pressure in the cooker is completely down, and
might open it too soon and scald yourself. New gauges are
available (they are standard in thread size).

Somewhere on the lid of the canner there should be a
safety valve (a small metal rod encased in a rubber seal). If
the pressure in the canner gets dangerously high, this is supposed to blow out and release the steam, keeping the canner
from exploding. The rod should be loose and you should be
able to jiggle it up and down with your finger. I would *not*
recommend that you buy any model which does not have a
safety valve.

If there is a small pipe sticking out of the lid of the

canner, there should be a pressure regulator with that model canner. The pressure regulator is a small metal weight which fits on top of this small pipe. (Mel calls it the "wibble wobble.") This is designed to rock gently when the pressure reaches fifteen pounds. By the way, the pressure regulator on my Presto *canner* is the same as the one on my Presto pressure *cooker.*

Open up the canner. It should have a rubber sealing ring fitting into a groove around the inside of the canner's lid. This should be in good condition: these are readily available for many models.

The pressure canner should also have a wire rack or basket into which the jars may be put during processing. If this is missing, you may be able to improvise one, or perhaps the one from your hot water bath canner will fit, so it is not as important. Again, Presto will supply the wire rack for its pressure canners separately. Some sort of rack *must* be used, however. Jars set right on the pot bottom would crack during the canning operation.

If you have bought a used canner, it is probably a good idea to have the pressure gauge checked. This may be done through a local vocational school, agricultural college, extension agent (ask your state representative or department of agriculture how to get hold of him . . . or look in the *Old Farmer's Almanac*), or gas or electric company. Get the gauge checked again every year.

The pressure canner can also be used as an ordinary pressure cooker. Because it is metal it should not be used for pickling, winemaking or brewing. I find it very useful for cooking down soup stock.

OTHER USEFUL UTENSILS: A *wide-necked funnel* is extremely convenient. This is a funnel with a neck just wide enough to fit into a regular-mouthed canning jar. It enables you to fill the jars without messing the food onto the jar's rim.

My local grocery store sells them, as does any store that sells housewares and canning supplies. My mother-in-law has a wide-necked funnel which has a number of strainers of various degrees of fineness as inserts. If you see one of these, grab it! I would give anything to have one! If I had one, my tomato juice would be free of the tiny little seeds which got through my food mill.

A *food mill* is extremely handy to have around. It is useful not only for puréeing food for canning, but for preparation of baby food, mashed potatoes, etc.

A *number of large pots* with lids for precooking food. Especially convenient is a "blancher" (also called a spaghetti cooker). A blancher is a large pot with a lid and a separate colander that fits into the pot. If your recipe calls for precooking food, you remove the colander, fill it with the food, bring your water to a boil, put the colander in the pot. When your cooking time is up you lift out the colander and you don't have to fish around for each and every spoonful of food. It is useful in freezing as well as in ordinary cooking. They come in metal or agate. Get the agate ones so you can use them for winemaking and pickling as well. They cost about seven dollars. Two are three times as useful as one.

A *kitchen scale* is one of the more necessary items to have around.

Measuring cups and spoons.

Getting Down to Business: Canning Food

I was lucky. When I felt like learning canning I merely had to ask my mother-in-law, who had been canning successfully for years. We spent a number of weeks one summer canning together, enabling me to get over my initial shyness about possibly doing something wrong, with all the dire consequences that might set in motion.

That's really the most comfortable way to learn canning —do it with someone who has done it before. But if that's not possible, there's nothing to keep you from doing it yourself. It's not all that complicated.

If you are doing it alone for the first time, you will have to be extra methodical and systematic. I strongly suggest that you read through a number of instructions for canning, and a variety of recipes so you get a feeling for the process. I have found that this is an extremely effective method of learning any new form of cooking—read an entire cookbook or two through to get the "flavor" of the cooking style, then go on and try individual recipes.

Let me describe in detail what I do when I can food, and, incidentally, give a few recipes along the way.

One summer while we were berrying, Mel's father and I found a wild pear tree literally covered with pears. You couldn't see the branches for the pears. It was quite a sight. They were little pears, not very good for eating out of hand, but excellent for canning and pickling. We picked a shopping bag full.

When we got home the first thing I had to do was sort them over. They were still pretty green, and needed some ripening up before processing. So I transferred the pears to a bushel basket, looking each one over for rotten spots that might contaminate the rest as they ripened. These I set aside. I also set aside those with breaks in the skin, and without stems. The little hole where the stem should have been lets air into the fruit, providing an excellent place for rot to start. Any pears that seemed riper than the others I also set aside. Those set aside would require more active watching.

Then I let the pears sit. Since they were quite green at first I would sort them over once a week, again removing to bowls the ripest of the fruit, and transfer the rest to another basket. This is necessary since those at the bottom of the basket tend to ripen up faster than the ones at the top.

Since I was going to can the fruit I wanted them to be quite firm, but sweet. I had the deuce of a time figuring out how to tell when they were ripe for canning until it finally occurred to me to eat a few at various stages. I found out pretty quickly what they should look like.

When I had a good number of pears ready for canning, I proceeded in the following manner:

Here's a recipe of the sort to be found in the canning section of any good cookbook. Notice the recipe includes how to prepare the food, how to pack it, and how to process it. This is the usual format of any canning recipe.

> *Pears, cold-pack method. Wash, peel, halve and core pears. Pack cut-side down into hot jars, cover with boiling syrup to within 1/2" of top, adjust lids. Process in boiling water bath 25 minutes for pints, 30 minutes for quarts; or at 5 pounds pressure for 10 minutes.*

First I cleared the decks for action. I would need my sink and all the counterspace I could get. I emptied my dish rack so I would have a place to set clean canning jars and put down a towel on a heat resistant counter so I would have a space to set the hot jars after processing. (If I didn't use the towel, the hot jars might crack when I set them on the cold counter after processing.) For this batch I decided to use my hot water canner, so I washed it up, then washed up a mess of jars, rinsed them well by turning them upside down and spraying into them with the sink spray. For the first batch I used dome-lidded mason jars, so I counted out the number of lids I would need for the first canner load, separated the screw bands from the disk lids, and discarded the protective paper. I put the disk lids in a small pot with water to cover and boiled them gently for a couple of minutes (this is called scalding—it softens up the rubber circle on the lid, enabling it to seal better). I left the lids in the hot water until I was ready to use them. I put hot water in the same number of canning jars and set these aside. I put the rack in the canner, then put in a few inches of hot water so I could set the jars in right after packing and keep the full ones from cooling down while I packed the rest. I was going to pack the pears in a medium heavy sugar syrup, so I started a large kettle of it heating in the proportion of one cup sugar to two cups water. (This was still a trifle sweet for us, I realized when I tasted the syrup, so I added more water. Taste as you go along. Also, keep records!) I also set my tea kettle full of water to boil in case I needed to make extra syrup in a hurry.

The initial preparations made, I was now ready to deal with the pears.

The first thing was to wash them. I filled a large pot with water, then I proceeded to peel, halve and core them, putting the prepared pears in a large pot of water to which a dash of vinegar had been added (you can use lemon juice, or a tablespoon of salt instead) to keep the peeled pears from discoloring. I set aside the peelings and cores for making jell, pear sauce or soda syrup later, also in vinegar water.

When I had close to what I thought would fill a canner full of jars, I started packing. I placed the pear halves cut-side down in the jar, first emptying out the hot water, of course; getting in as many as I could, but stopping about an inch from the top of the jar. When a jar was packed with pears, I filled it with boiling syrup to within half an inch of the top, slid a butter knife down the inside of the jar, and jiggled the pears a little until the air bubbles stopped rising. I added syrup to make up for the settling, put the disk lid on, then tightened the screw band firmly without forcing it. (If you spill while filling the jar, you should wipe the rim before putting the cap on so no food particle keeps it from sealing.) Then that jar

went into the canner and the next jar was packed. When the
canner was full I put it on the stove with a fire under it, put
enough hot (*not* boiling) water in the canner to cover the
jars, put the lid on, and waited for it to come to a boil. When
it did, I wrote down what time I should turn it off (I have a
devil of a time remembering). They were quarts so I had to
keep them boiling for half an hour, adding water if enough
boiled away to expose the jar lids. At the end of the half hour,
I turned off the heat, fished out the handles of the canner
rack with a fork, lifted the rack part way out, and hooked it
onto the sides of the canner. The jars were then sticking out
of the water so I could grab each one with a pot holder (*not*
by the lid—I didn't want to break the seal), and set it to cool
on the towel I had laid out. Since I had a window open in the
kitchen and a draft might cause the jars to cool unevenly and
crack, I put a towel over the cooling jars. There they had to
sit for twenty-four hours, when they would be thoroughly
cooled and sealed. Periodically, while the jars were cooling
and contracting, I would hear soft "pops," which meant that
the dome lids were being sucked slightly inward from the
vacuum created by the contraction of the jars' contents, and
the seal was being effected.

While one batch was processing, I scalded more lids and
started preparing and packing for the next load.

After twenty-four hours of cooling, I checked the seals
on the jars. I did this by first looking at the disk lid carefully
to see that it was slightly curved inward. I removed the screw
band (which might be quite loose from the jar's contraction
during cooking, by the way . . . don't let it upset you) and
tapped the disk lid with the hind end of the spoon. The sound
should have been, and was in each case, high pitched. If it
was a low-pitched, dull sound (clunk versus ping) it would
mean the vacuum was not as good as it should be. As a final
check (the most important one, in fact) I turned the jar up-

side down to see if it leaked. If the jars hadn't passed these tests, I would have used them immediately or reprocessed them. Since they had in fact sealed, I wiped them off (they sometimes get sticky during canning), replaced the screw bands, labeled and stored them away. (You can leave off the screw bands if you like and use them for other jars. The disk lids are available separately.)

What I have described is a "cold pack" where the food is packed cold into hot jars, covered with boiling water, syrup or brine, covered and processed. Now for a "hot pack."

> *Herbal Pears, hot pack method. Wash pears, removing flower ends but leaving stems. Peel if desired. Drop a few at a time into boiling syrup. Return to a boil, then cook one to two minutes depending on the ripeness and size of fruit. Put a few sprigs of herb into hot jars, pack in the hot pears, and add more herbs if desired. Fill with boiling syrup to within 1/2″ of top. Adjust lids. Process in boiling water bath 20 minutes for pints, 25 minutes for quarts; or at 5 pounds pressure for 8 minutes.*

When another batch of pears was ripe enough for canning I had recipes for minted pears, but no fresh mint. So I decided to experiment.

What I wanted was a fancy dessert. I had sage and summer savory growing in my garden, so I decided to make sage pears and savory pears, inventions of my own, by using these herbs in place of mint. The sage pears were good, but the savory pears were exquisite!

I made the same initial preparations as before. This time I decided to use some glass-lidded, clamp-style jars, and the pressure canner. So when I washed up the jars I also washed up the glass lids and set these in a pot of hot water to await use. I made sure that when I washed the pressure canner I did not immerse the pressure gauge in water since that would wreck it. Also, instead of getting out dome lids, I got out the appropriate-size jar rubbers and scalded these the same way I had scalded the dome lids.

I washed the pears, removing the little flower end, but leaving on the stems. (The flower end is not poisonous, it is merely that in cooking it would fall apart and fleck the syrup with unsightly black spots.) Again I put the prepared pears in vinegar water until I was ready to cook them.

I made up my syrup (medium again—this was just to our taste for the herbal pears, as it turned out), and brought it to a boil. Then I dropped the pears a few at a time (no more than could easily float on top) into the boiling syrup, let it come to a boil and boiled it for one minute. (If the pears had been greener, they would have had to boil longer to soften up, and if they had been large, they would have needed more time to heat them through.) Meanwhile, I emptied a canning jar and put in a few sprigs of summer savory. At the end of the precooking time, I fished the pears out gently with a slotted spoon and packed them into a jar, occasionally putting in another sprig or two of savory. When the jar was packed to within an inch of the top, I filled it to within a half inch of the top with boiling syrup (in which the pears had been precooked), jiggled the fruit with a butter knife to release air bubbles, and added any necessary syrup to make up the required amount. Then I fished out a jar rubber, gave it a good pull (the way you do when you want to limber up a stiff rubber band), and stretched it to fit around the top of the jar so that it laid flat on the little ledge of glass provided for it. When I did this I tried to remember to put the little pull-tab on the jar rubber on the opposite side from the wire clamp so it would not interfere with clamping the lid down. Then I put on the glass lid.

The wire clamp jar has two sections in the lock. I fit the larger of the two wires over the glass lid, resting it in the little groove in the center of the lid. In order to do this the shorter, rounded wire (often called the "bail") must be placed in its upward position. This is the way it goes into the canner. (Since the jar is not tightly closed during the processing, the air will be forced out of the jar as its contents boil, and the vacuum seal will be all the better.) It sounds complicated, but the first time you handle one of these jars you'll easily see how they work.

As I fill each jar, I put it in the wire rack in the pressure canner, into which I have already put the amount of hot water the manufacturer recommended (my canner takes two quarts). The canner lid goes on loosely so the heat stays in while I pack the other jars.

When the pressure canner is full, I make sure the actual front of the canner is to the front of the stove (it is marked). I check that the vent pipe is clear and the safety valve rod can be jiggled up and down freely. I then close the pressure canner according to the manufacturer's directions, and start the heat going full blast.

Canners differ. On my canner this is the procedure I have to follow. I put the heat on full until the steam begins pouring out of the open vent pipe. I adjust the flame to the lowest point where the steam continues to come out steadily. I let it "vent" for ten minutes (this gets the air out of the canner and jars). I then put the pressure regulator on the vent pipe, raise the flame as high as it will go, and watch the rod on the safety valve push to its upward position and the pressure gauge begin to rise. When it reaches five pounds pressure I lower the flame and sit and watch it for eight minutes, regulating the flame slightly if the pressure goes above or below the necessary five pounds. If the phone rings, to hell with it. At the end of the eight minutes, I turn off the heat and let the pressure fall of its own accord. When the pressure gauge reaches zero *and* the safety valve rod has lowered *(not before)*, I take off the pressure regulator, wait a couple of minutes to let it cool down more, then turn the lid of the pressure canner to its open position and lift it up and *away* from me so that the remnants of the steam don't get in my face (at this point the steam is unpleasantly but not dangerously hot). I give it another moment, then lift the jars out of the canner using pot holders, again *not by the lids,* for fear of breaking the seal. As each jar is taken out, I snap the curved bail wire down against the side of the jar into its final position (see illustration). This puts greater pressure on the jar rubber, helping it to seal. If the wire comes down easily and without a snap, it means that the pressure on the jar rubber won't be great enough. In such a case I put a piece of folded cardboard between the glass lid and the wire resting on it, releasing the clamp in order to do this (the boxes in which the jar rubbers come are just the thing for this— match book covers also work well). This final snapping down of the clamp completes the canning process. Again I set the jars aside to cool, covered with a towel if the room is drafty. Twenty-four hours later, I invert them to make sure they have sealed properly. If they leak, it means they haven't sealed and the food must be used immediately or packed and processed over again.

Canning recipes are readily available, for free or at a very minimal cost (see bibliography). I've found the best recipe collections come from the manuals that come with canners, from the manufacturers of canning supplies (in this part of the country, Ball and Kerr are the main ones), and from the U.S. Department of Agriculture. There are, by the way, slight differences in recommended processing times from these sources. All of the recipes I've tried from these sources work very well, however.

You can vary canning recipes within certain limits. Keep these principles in mind, however:

1. *Do not* vary the style of pack (hot or cold) in recommended processing time. For some foods a cold pack requires extra processing time. There are things you can vary, however.
2. Fruits and vegetables may be canned in plain water, in their precooking liquid, with or without sugar, pure salt, herbs, spices to taste. It is not the salt, sugar, etc., that does the preserving, but the heat. Vinegar or lemon juice may be added to any recipe for flavor or to stabilize color as desired. *Only* use *pure* salt in canning, or your liquid might get cloudy.
3. A clove of garlic, and up to a teaspoon of chopped hot or sweet pepper or onion may be added for flavoring to each quart without change in the processing time.
4. Vegetables or fruits may be mixed in the same jar. The recipe for the ingredient requiring the *longest* processing time should be followed for the mixture, however. If you are hot packing, precook the different vegetables separately according to their recipe; then mix, pack and process according to the one requiring the longest time and highest pressure.

Using Home Canned Food

To open the glass-lidded, wire-clamp-style canning jar, release the wire clamp by pulling up on the part that is against the side of the jar, then push aside the wire on top of the jar, and pull the tab on the jar rubber. I can't pull hard enough to break the seal unaided, so I pull with a pair of pliers. As the seal breaks there is a slight sucking in of air. The glass lid comes off easily once the seal is broken. Some people slit the pull tab on the jar rubber and pull; I prefer my pliers. Discard the rubber.

To open the dome-lidded mason jars, unscrew the screw band and remove it, then pry up the metal disk lid. I have a little gadget, a flat metal jar opener, called a "vacuum jar lifter," which I find very handy. If you see one get it. Again, there will be a slight sucking in of air as the seal breaks.

Canned fruits (including tomatoes) may be used as they come from the jar. Canned vegetables and meats, however, *must* be boiled fifteen minutes before tasting.

Store canned goods in a cool, dark place if possible. Try to keep them from freezing . . . if they freeze, the jars might crack. If you store them in light, the contents of the jars might fade. If you can't manage a dark storage place, you may use the old-fashioned technique of wrapping each jar in newspaper.

A Final Note on Canning

Since I have come across a certain misconception repeatedly, I might as well say something about it in case you come across it, too. I have been solemnly assured by people who know nothing about it, that they have it on the best of authorities that tomatoes are the most dangerous thing to can! That if you can tomatoes, you are sure to get botulism. This is nonsense. Tomatoes, because of their high acid content, are among the *safest* and easiest things to can, which is why they are listed in canning manuals (including government pamphlets) in the recipe section dealing with *fruits*. There is no way, repeat, no way, you can get botulism from a can of tomatoes, whether processed at home or in a factory. Actually, I suspect I know the source of the myth about the dangers of canning tomatoes. Back in the good old days, before it was really understood what caused food spoilage, much canning was done by the so-called "open-kettle" method. This method called for cooking the food for a number of hours in a kettle, then packing into hot jars, sealing and storing without further processing. During packing, of course, the food was exposed to air, and could easily pick up yeasts and other bacteria from the atmosphere. Now, tomatoes are one of the foods most loved by yeasts, which is why tomato yeast bread is such a light, airy affair. The result of sealing tomatoes plus yeast in a jar was described by an Italian friend of mine:

A couple she knew in Italy lived part of the year in the country, and part of the year in Rome. Every year the lady of the house would put up tomatoes galore to serve during the winter months. One year she brought her canned tomatoes to her Rome apartment, and went off on a shopping trip for a couple of days, leaving her husband at home in the apartment. In the middle of the night her husband heard an explosion. He rushed into the kitchen and found tomatoes all over the ceiling, the walls, and everything else. He got out of the room just as another jar went off. He called the fire department and left the apartment, not returning for two days, when the mess had been cleared away. The yeast had begun multiplying and producing carbon dioxide, just as in beer and soda. The pressure had exploded the jars, which were not designed to withhold that kind of pressure.

I have heard other stories of exploding jars of tomatoes: but they are all old stories, coming from the time when open-kettle canning was an accepted practice. These days, and for this reason, open-kettle canning is *not recommended.* Since you are now packing and processing your food in closed containers, all the yeasts and bacteria in the food are destroyed, and those from the air cannot get at the food, so there is no danger of this sort of thing occurring. The only foods that *may* be canned by the open-kettle method are: jellies and jams (their very high sugar contents make them so thick that yeasts, etc., cannot work on them); some pickles (the high vinegar content protects them . . . yeasts cannot work in a high concentration of acetic acid); and chutneys (the high sugar *and* high acetic acid content protects them).

The moral of the story is: (1) tomatoes are safe to can; and (2) don't use the open-kettle canning method for foods other than the above even if an old-timer tells you she's been canning by the open-kettle method without disaster for years!

CHAPTER 7

JELLIES
AND JAMS

Greer speaking

I used to despise parents who fed their children peanut butter and jelly sandwiches. I had been brought up to believe that this American favorite was not food, but merely filler without food value. Since I've moved to the country, however, I've been learning a bit of history and nutrition, and also have learned my mistake. It turns out that peanuts are almost as good a source of protein as meat. And "jell" (the generic term for jellies and jams) was for a long time an important means of supplying fruit to the winter diet.

Around here jell is not confined to morning toast, or to the inevitable peanut butter and jelly sandwich. It is used in baking and is also served in slices with roasts the way cranberry sauce is on Thanksgiving. My urban prejudices were completely dispersed when I tasted homemade jells and

121

found they need not be cloyingly sweet like the commercial products.

How It Works

Jell is made by cooking up a high-acid, pectin-containing fruit with sugar (I'll explain about pectin in a minute). After a certain amount of cooking, the pectin reacts with the sugar and acid and causes the mixture to thicken. At this point the brew is spooned into jars and cooled. As it cools it congeals and the result is jelly (if fruit juice is used) or jam (if the whole chopped or mashed fruit is used). If it is not cooked long enough, it will not jell and the result will be fruit syrup. If it is cooked too long the result will strongly resemble gum drops, but will still be edible.

Pectin is a substance that is found in varying degrees in fruits, especially unripe and underripe fruits. Some fruits contain a lot of pectin (apples, currants and cranberries, for example). Others, like elderberries, don't have much.

From fruits naturally low in pectin, or from fully ripe fruits, jellies and jams may be made by adding pectin. I know of and use two kinds of commercially packed fruit pectin: Sure-Jell, which is powdered and comes packaged like Jello; and Certo, which is liquid and comes in a measured bottle, making it marginally easier to use for odd-sized batches. In every container of pectin there is an excellent recipe pamphlet. The main drawbacks of using the commercially packed pectin are, jell made with it requires considerably more sugar than does jell made without it, and it may contain preservatives.

An alternative to using commercially packed pectin is to add an equal measure of high pectin fruit to low pectin fruit. I will describe both methods.

What You Need

A large pot suitable for top-of-the-stove cooking. A blancher (see canning chapter) is about the right size. As usual, an agate (enameled) one is best.

A wooden spoon for stirring.

A metal spoon for skimming.

Large bowls come in handy, as does an enameled colander.

A kitchen scale, measuring cups and spoons.

Rock (optional).

Jelly bag (a triangular cloth bag open at the top) for straining fruit mash. Make it of flannel (nap side in) or muslin. A pillow case will do. Another straining technique uses flat pieces of muslin, flannel, cheesecloth, or a lightweight new diaper.

An old coffee pot (the smaller the better) for melting the paraffin.

Jelly jars. Any jar or glass can be used as a jelly jar. You will want some kind of lid, but if the jars you have handy don't come with lids, you can make them out of aluminum foil or waxed paper and they will store quite well. The screw-on baby food jars and other recycled supermarket jars that seal can be used without paraffin if the jell is packed *boiling hot* and covered immediately. There are two styles of jelly jars available commercially. One type consists of little canning jars with ordinary dome lids or sometimes one piece screw-on lids. These seal without paraffin, and so are the most convenient. They are flared upwards so you can get the jell out in one piece for fancy serving. The other style have loosely fitting metal slip-on lids designed to protect a paraffin seal. If you are buying new jelly jars, get the dome-lidded ones.

Preparing the Fruit

Jams use chopped or mashed fruit (without peels and pits). First clean the fruit thoroughly, discarding any bad spots—stems, and the flower ends. Then peel and core or pit the fruit where appropriate. These peels, cores and pits contain pectin, so if you will not be using Certo or Sure-Jell, boil them up with a little water for a few minutes. Strain off the liquid and pour it over the rest of the fruit, which in the meanwhile you have cut into smallish pieces. Put it all into a kettle over a *very low* flame (you don't want to cook the fruit just yet—you want to soften it) and mash it with a potato masher, or squeeze it with your hands. For the dryish, mealy fruits (like apples and pears), add enough water to keep it from burning. Pretty soon the fruit begins oozing juice and the pieces get pretty small. Now the concoction is ready for making jam.

If you want to make jelly instead of jam, put the mash into a jelly bag and hang it point down over a large bowl or agate kettle or a crock (don't use a metal container, the acid in the juice might react with it), and let it drip overnight. Or else put a number of layers of cheese cloth, a piece of muslin, or a lightweight diaper (this works very well) into a colander over your kettle, bowl or crock. Dump in the mash, cover it with a plate and let it drip over night. The mash looks (and feels) surprisingly dry when it is done dripping. If you are in a hurry, you may set a rock or jug of water on top of the mash, or you can squeeze the bag; but it will still take a number of hours to get the juice out. If you do squeeze, your jell will be cloudy with tiny bits of fruit fiber, resembling in texture a strained jam.

Another method of juicing fruit is to put it through a fruit or wine press (see Winemaking for details).

By the way, you can get more juice out of the mash. I

sometimes do the following. Say I have some elderberries. I juice them, allowing them to drip overnight without weights or squeezing. I make this juice, with added pectin, into a nice clear jell (elderberries don't have much pectin). Then I put the mash into a pot with half as much water as I got juice from the first dripping. I heat this to boiling, add some under-ripe apples, then put this through the jelly bag. From this second dripping I make elderberry-apple jell without added pectin.

Making Jelly or Jam Using Added Pectin

Jell made with added pectin is almost foolproof. Follow the recipes that come with the pectin exactly and you will end up with excellent jell. You might want to improve on the recipe—a little lemon juice or rhubarb will give tartness to an overly sweet concoction; a dash of brandy or vermouth will perk up bland tasting fruit. (If a fruit tastes bland you may be sure it will make a dull jelly or jam.) Juices may be mixed. If very few raspberries are available they may be stretched with apples. The possibilities are unlimited. What you may *not* do is change the cooking time, or the sugar-juice-pectin ratio of the recipe; nor may you eliminate the added acid entirely. If you are allergic to citrus fruit, however, you may replace lemon juice with cider vinegar. You may also substitute lime juice or grapefruit juice for the lemon.

A number of friends have begged me to put in this book my recipe for peach jam.

First I wash up the jelly glasses. Some people boil them for five minutes. This is probably a good idea since they won't be processed like canned foods are; but my mother-in-law doesn't boil them and I don't either. (There is no danger of food poisoning from jell so the precaution seems unwarranted. Mel says to put in that botulism is not a problem because of the high acid content of fruits. But use your own judgment about boiling the jars. If you don't boil them, though, scrub them well in very hot water.)

PEACH JAM

3 pounds peaches, peeled and chopped	6 1/2 cups sugar
4 tablespoons lemon juice	1 box Sure-Jell

I weigh out three pounds of fully ripe peaches. For jell made with added pectin use fully ripe fruit or your jell might come out too tough . . . remember, underripe fruit has significant pectin of its own. If you don't have fully ripe fruit, store it until it ripens up.

I wash, peel and pit the peaches. Then I chop them up until they begin to ooze juice and the pieces are pretty small. The recipe in the Sure-Jell box calls for mixing in 2 tablespoons of lemon juice: I increase this to 4 tablespoons as I don't like an overly sweet jam. I measure out 4 cups of the chopped peaches (if I don't have enough peaches, I add a little water or apple juice). I measure out 6 1/2 cups of sugar and set it aside. I put the peaches in the large agate kettle over a high heat and stir in the contents of one package of pectin. When the mixture comes to a full boil, I pour the sugar in and stir for dear life until it boils up again in spite of my stirring. (When it boils up, will it *ever* boil up. . . . make sure the kettle is much bigger than you think you will need!) Then I start timing it: it should boil wildly for one minute. At the end of the minute I turn off the heat, skim off all the foam that forms on top of the brew, stir and skim for five minutes. A metal spoon seems to work best for this. The stuff I skim off I put in a jar in the refrigerator for immediate use—it's a little sweeter, and not as pretty as the finished jam, but still quite edible. I then spoon the skimmed jam into *warm* jelly jars to within 1/4″ of the top. If they are dome-lidded jars, I wipe the rims and seal them immediately as in canning, but invert them once, as recommended. The same goes for baby-food jars and other recycled jars that reseal.

If they are plain glasses, or jars that don't reseal, they must be sealed with paraffin. Many supermarkets and most hardware stores sell paraffin.

I find the handiest thing for melting paraffin is an old one-cup coffee pot. I set it on the stove *in a pan of water* with just enough heat to keep the water simmering. The pan of water is a precaution. If you put the pot of paraffin directly over the flame beware of fire—be very careful indeed! Keep the fire low and watch it carefully. Turn the fire off before the last of the paraffin has melted, and let that last bit melt of its own accord. If the paraffin gets too hot it will burst into flame (candles are often made of paraffin, as Mel points out).

Mel puts in a plea, since I always make him remove the paraffin when I open a fresh jar of jell. "If the jar has a narrow neck, or tapers inward, fill it full enough so the wax is at the top of the jar and thin, otherwise the only way of getting it out is to cut it in half, and one half always sinks." This is very good advice, and I sometimes even follow it. I pour a little paraffin on the filled jars, then tilt the jar so the wax runs around over the top of the jam and the inside of the jar rim. When that sets (it turns white), I pour on a second thin coat of paraffin, again shifting the jar around to distribute the paraffin evenly. The end result should be 1/8″ paraffin.

When the filled jars have cooled I put on the lids, or cover them with aluminum foil, wipe them, label and date them, and store them away.

I use Sure-Jell for the peach jam merely from habit. Certo produces just as good a finished product. Follow the recipe in the pamphlet you find under the Certo label if you want to try it.

Here's an offbeat recipe that uses Certo.

SPICED ROSE PETAL WINE JELLY

2 cups Rose petal wine	6 allspice
1/2 bottle Certo	the contents of 6
2 3/4 cups sugar	cardamom pods
10 cloves	

Toast the spices in an ungreased frying pan over a high heat, shaking them constantly until they become fragrant (maybe half a minute). Tie them up in a small bag or a number of layers of cheesecloth. Mix the sugar, wine and spice bag in the top of a double boiler. Stir constantly until the sugar is dissolved (the syrup becomes clear). Remove from the heat and stir in 1/2 bottle of Certo. Pour into jelly jars and seal at once. Makes about five cups.

I used homemade rose petal wine (see Chapter 11 for the recipe), because the batch we made was too sweet for our taste as a wine. It makes a very pale pink, pleasant, and refreshing jell. You may use any wine and any combination of spices you like. For a dry wine use 3 cups of sugar to 2 cups wine.

NOTE: Most jell made with added pectin jells as it cools. Some, like elderberry, might take a couple of weeks of storage to jell properly, however. Don't worry if it seems liquid when it cools. If you followed the directions, chances are it will jell perfectly.

Making Jell from Scratch

Making jelly or jam without added pectin can be nerve-racking for a beginner. My two favorite examples are, first,

Louisa May Alcott's classic account of an unsuccessful jelly-making attempt in *Little Women*—leading to high drama in the form of Meg's first marital quarrel. The other is my mother-in-law's story of when she was newly wed, making apple jelly with *her* mother-in-law. She says they cooked it and cooked it all day long before they got it to jell. It was a *hot* summer day and she was *mad*. As she should have been. Jelly shouldn't take more than half an hour of cooking. And a little know-how (borrowed if necessary). And a sense of humor (acquired if necessary). And a willingness to be versatile (if worse comes to worst).

After all, jelly that won't jell makes excellent syrup for making sodas, flavoring milk, eating with pancakes or ice cream, glazing roasts. So the stakes aren't very high.

The borrowed know-how consists mainly of two things: evaluating the fruit, and the jelly test. First the fruit.

When making jelly with added pectin use fully ripe fruit. When making jelly from scratch use *underripe* fruit with a sprinkling of *unripe* fruit. Then it will jell, and in a reasonable amount of time. With fully ripe fruit you *might* get it to jell, but then again, you might not. And I'm not one of those people who feel using added pectin is "cheating." I look at the fruit I have available and decide on that basis how to go about it.

It took me awhile to catch on about the jelly test. The first time I made jell without added pectin I did it by accident. A friend gave me some raspberry juice she had made. I had just run out of strawberry syrup (my daughter likes it in her morning milk) and decided to treat her to raspberry syrup. I boiled up the raspberry juice with an equal amount of sugar and a dash of lemon (to keep the color stable) for five minutes. It seemed to thicken up, but I didn't give it a thought. Raspberries are supposedly low in pectin. What I forgot was that the pectin content of fruit varies from year to year. Our rainy, cold spring that year seemed to enhance the pectin content of raspberries. I poured it into a warm grape juice bottle. And it jelled. It was quite a job getting it out of the bottle. So I decided it was easy making jelly without added pectin.

The second time I tried I wasn't as successful, or so I thought. I decided to make blackberry jam. I put the nice ripe blackberries in an agate kettle with a low fire under it and mashed them until they were soggy. Then I put the mash through a food mill to sift out the largest of the seeds, measured the result in a measuring cup and cooked it up with three quarters of that amount of sugar. And I cooked it. And forty-five minutes later, I was still cooking it.

I couldn't seem to catch on about the jelly test. Unfortunately it is one of those things you have to see once to recognize. Descriptions just don't do it. What is supposed to happen is this: While you are cooking the jell you periodically dip out a spoonful, let it cool for a moment, then pour it slowly back into the pot. The syrup, or so say the experts, is supposed to at first drip off the spoon in two drops; when the jell is almost ready, the two drops should merge into one (this is called "sheeting"). I couldn't get it to drip off in two drops, much less one. But after forty-five minutes it sort of thickened up, the way the raspberry juice had, so I decided to hell with it. I packed it into hot jars, sealed it and set it on the window sill figuring the sun would cook it a bit more. After a few days I stored it away. A month later I had occasion to open a jar and it was still mushy, but it firmed up when I put it in the refrigerator. Three months later I opened another jar and found that it had jelled perfectly.

Which brings me to the point: some jells don't firm up right away. Sometimes placing the jars in the sun, or just plain aging will do the trick on underdone jells. My mistake, of course, was to use fully ripe fruit. I hadn't got a "jelly test" even after forty-five minutes because I hadn't cooked it enough to concentrate the pectin.

What I would do now in such a case is add a little more sugar if it didn't jell in, say, twenty minutes. If that didn't do it, I would either remake it with added pectin, or hope aging would do the trick—consoling myself with the variety of uses I could put it to if it stayed liquid.

A substitute for the spoon jelly test is a cold saucer jelly test. Put a whole stack of saucers in the refrigerator before you start. Then when you think the jell might be near done, drip a few drops on a cold saucer and return it to the refrigerator. If it runs around the saucer when you tilt it, it's not done. If the jell doesn't run, you're almost there. Another minute of cooking (and this minute *is* important) then it is ready.

A less important hint, but one convenient to know, is this: If you want your jelly or jam to jell faster, and you're making it from scratch, preheat the sugar. Put it in the oven at 150° or so for fifteen or twenty minutes before you start cooking the jell. It really works!

Any decently comprehensive cookbook will give the standard recipes for jelly and jam—*Fannie Farmer* and *The Joy of Cooking* are outstanding examples. Once you've tried a few of the standard recipes "by the book," you might try improvising within the following rules:

For one cup of fruit juice or pulp, use 3/4 cup sugar (or slightly more, to taste; but no less). For very sour fruits, use equal amounts of sugar and juice. (Don't use more sugar than juice or it may not jell.)

To low-pectin fruits add underripe high-pectin fruits in a one–one proportion. For instance, *to* cherries, elderberries, strawberries, or pineapple *add* grapes, apples, currants, gooseberries, plums or cranberries.

To test for pectin content, put one tablespoon of the chilled juice into a glass. Add one tablespoon of grain alcohol. Swish it around so they mix, then let it sit for a few minutes. If it congeals, forming a single blob of jelly, the fruit is very high in pectin. If two softer blobs are formed the juice is moderately high in pectin. (It will jell, but it will take a little longer, and might require a little extra sugar.) If it doesn't congeal, or jells very loosely, it is low in pectin and should be mixed with another juice or used with commercially packed pectin. DO NOT TASTE THE RESULT—IT IS POISONOUS. DISCARD IT AND CLEANSE THE GLASS. The government requires by law that poisons be added to grain alcohol so people don't use it to get drunk with. When you hear of a child getting accidentally poisoned by drinking the stuff, don't blame fate, blame the government and the liquor lobby. But back to the rules of jelly making.

For best results, cook jell in small quantities (about four cups of fruit or fruit juice at a time). The less actual cooking time, the better tasting and healthier the jell will be.

Lemon, wine, brandy, or vermouth may be added to taste to flavor jell. One to four tablespoons per batch should do it.

Herbal flavorings may be added by one of two methods. Either bruise the leaves of a bunch of mint, lemon verbena, tarragon, basil, savory, or whatever your favorite herb is, and wave it around in the kettle as you're cooking the jell until it reaches the desired strength. Or drop a sprig of the herb in each jelly jar and pour the hot jell over it.

To spice jell, toast those sweet spices (cloves, cardamom, cinnamon, allspice, mace, ginger) in an ungreased frying pan, shaking it constantly, until the spices become fragrant (about half a minute). Tie the spices into a small bag or a number of layers of cheesecloth and add it to the jell while it's cooking. Remove it when the jell tastes good.

You may freeze or can fruit or fruit juice for out-of-season jell making. Either don't add sugar, or record how much sugar you are using so you don't run into difficulty with proportions.

There are other methods of making jell which I have not tried. One is a method of cooking the jell in the sun for a number of days rather than on top of the stove. Jell made this way is supposed to be especially fragrant and fruity. It is described by Euell Gibbons in his exciting book *Stalking the Wild Asparagus,* in the wild strawberry section. A modified sun-cooking method is detailed by Catherine Plagemann in her lovely book *Fine Preserving,* also under strawberries.

There are also "freezer jells"—so called because while they require very little cooking and thus retain a truer aroma and flavor, they will not store well except in a deep freeze. Freezer space is always at a premium in our house, so I haven't used the technique. Euell Gibbons gives recipes for these jells in a number of his books and the Sure-Jell and Certo recipe pamphlets both have sections on freezer jells.

CHAPTER 8

FREEZING FOOD

Greer speaking

From the time we moved in, I had my heart set on owning a freezer. I'd discovered a freezer's advantages during our brief life in Yonkers (one came with the house). So I kept pestering Mel to turn us up a freezer.

At first we thought we'd get a used one. But that worried me: if I was going to put better than $400 worth of meat into the freezer, not to mention vegetables and fruits, I wasn't going to take chances. So we bought a big twenty-cubic-foot chest-type freezer from Montgomery Ward. For a first freezer and a limited budget, I'd really recommend a chest-type freezer. More fits into one, even if it is not very handy getting stuff out of it. But at some point or other, I'd dearly love to get a second, smaller freezer, an upright with a quick-freeze shelf or two. (By the way, I'm sorry now that I bought a new freezer: the new ones all seem to be plastic. Mel's aunt has one, and *broke* it by dropping some frozen meat on it, if you can imagine! And it doesn't retain cold as well come a power failure . . . but more about that later.)

Once we had the freezer, the next question was where to put it. We set it up in the shed attached to the house (there's a door from the kitchen, so it was very handy). Mel's mother keeps her freezer in an enclosed, but unheated patio. Another couple we know keep both their freezers in an unheated barn. This way they can take advantage of winter cold weather to help keep their food frozen. But these are older models. While I have since found out that *some* newer models don't have to be kept from freezing, the instruction book for our freezer is very explicit about the fact that the freezer should not be allowed to freeze! (Check on this point when you are shopping around for a freezer.) So we had to move the freezer inside.

But keep the freezer out of the kitchen if possible. It is the warmest room of the house, summer and winter. (And if it is the chest-style freezer and has a little drain on the bottom, put the freezer up on blocks so that you can stuff a pan under the drain when you defrost the fool thing.)

I try not to open the freezer more than once a day. Each time the freezer is opened it is warmed up and up goes the electric bill and down goes the food quality. I also try to keep the freezer well stocked. It is a waste of good electricity to run a near-empty freezer. Also, in case of a power failure the food will last longer if the freezer is full—each item is storing some of that precious cold. Speaking of blackouts, if there is one, pile blankets on the freezer for insulation (do not cover the ventilating hole, however) and DON'T OPEN THE FREEZER unless it is to put in dry ice (advisable if the blackout lasts more than a day or two for older models, and, believe it or not, only twelve hours for my new, improved model!). Get dry ice from an ice cream factory or freezing plant. Handle it with gloves, because it burns. Put cardboard between it and the food. Of course, if it's cold outside and there's a chance your frozen food might thaw, you can move the food to a shady spot outside to keep it frozen, but dry ice will keep it colder, so it is infinitely preferable. The quality of frozen food depends on, among other things, its being kept at 0°F or a little below, with very little *variation* in temperature.

If your food does thaw, cook it all up and eat the best of it, and refreeze the remainder as cooked food if the power has returned. If not, can the food: to can frozen food, heat it through, and follow a recipe for hot-packing. If the food only partially thaws (still has ice crystals in it) it can be refrozen.

I take advantage of this last fact when I buy bulk ready-frozen fruit from places like Agway. I bought thirty pounds each of cherries, rhubarb and pineapple last year. They came frozen *solid* in big tins. I was mighty perplexed about what to do about it until Mel's mother told me to let them thaw just enough to be able to break apart the fruit and repack it in small containers. I did this with the pineapple and the rhubarb and it worked very well. I had already canned up the cherries; that worked very well too.

What You Need for Efficient Freezing

A *freezer*, obviously. To my taste the bigger the better. Other people say plan between six and ten cubic feet of freezer space for each member of the family, depending on how much of your own food you grow, and whether you plan to freeze baked goods as well as meat, vegetables and fruits.

Freezer containers. You'll need a lot of these. The large mail order houses like Sears and Ward's sell the plastic ones very cheaply, as does Agway. I'm not talking about the 79¢ a piece variety that fancy supermarkets sell. We pay up to a dime per container. These containers are reusable and are conveniently marked as measuring cups. Be sure and get the rectangular ones. The round ones are uneconomical and inconvenient to use in the long run. You can't get as many of them in your freezer, and you can't pack certain foods in them efficiently (ever try getting asparagus spears into Cool Whip containers?).

Can-or-freeze jars may be used, but be SURE (!!!) not to overfill them, or these glass jars will break. The plastic containers only pop their lids.

Another alternative is to save waxed cardboard boxes in which commercially frozen foods come. These can be folded and stored for reuse if carefully handled. They will last a surprisingly long time if treated with care. My mother-in-law has some she's been using for the past ten years! However, with these boxes it is necessary either to line them with plastic bags, or to wrap the filled boxes with freezer paper, because they "sweat," and will dry out the food and allow air in. I have no patience with this sort of thing, and I hate to wash plastic bags, so I don't use them much.

Don't buy those fancy automatic machines that wrap and seal the food in plastic bags. They are expensive and frustrating, as well as wasteful. You're bound to run out of the plastic at particularly inconvenient times and will end up buying freezer containers anyway.

Treat with care whatever disposable aluminum cake tins come your way. But if you are going to buy them, buy real baking tins—they last longer and can stand rougher treatment—and they can be picked up easily at rummage and garage sales. I use both sorts for freezing combination dishes (such as "TV" dinners) for freezer-to-oven dinners.

The disposable items you will need are freezer paper and freezer tape for wrapping and sealing meat. (Waxed paper does not fill the bill here. It sweats, falls apart, and the bones poke through too easily.) Aluminum foil is expensive, but can be used in emergencies. Freezer tape is designed to stay sticky at very low temperatures. I've tried a few brands, and find the only one that really does the job is that sold by Sears. My experience is that the other ones fall off if brushed, a very inconvenient tendency indeed. A grease pencil or magic marker is useful for labeling.

You will need a *timer,* or an easy-to-read clock with a second hand. Also a couple of dish pans come in handy. The square plastic ones are best if you are using the square freezer containers. We have one of these, and use the baby's bathtub as a second.

A *large slotted spoon* is also convenient. Other necessary items are good knives, a cutting board for preparing food, plenty of space, and *plenty of ice.* Collect ice cube trays. You'll use them. Keep a plastic bag or two full of ice cubes in the freezer just in case some food you want to preserve turns up unexpectedly. And it will, especially when you get to know your gardening neighbors!

If you don't have one already, get yourself a *blancher,* described on page 108. You can improvise temporarily with a large stew pot and a frying basket.

You might want to make yourself a little mitre box for cutting up vegetables to the size of your freezer containers. You can do this by constructing or finding a topless wooden box which is open at one end. Saw out slits in the sides at appropriate intervals. Asparagus, broccoli, string beans, or whatever, are placed lengthwise in the box and are cut by drawing a knife through the appropriate slot. I'm not that neat about it, I'm afraid.

Freezing Raw Meat

We devote between half to two-thirds of our freezer space to meat. When I first got my own freezer, I was determined to start buying my meat by the side—that is, half a steer at a time. I began pouring through all the cookbooks in the house and carefully studied diagrams of what came from where on sides of beef, pork, veal and lamb. My mother-in-law caught me at it and laughed. "Why don't you just ask the butcher?" she asked. She gave me the name of the wholesale butcher she buys from, and who, as I knew from many delicious meals at her house, always gave her good meat. So I called him up and made an appointment. He told me to come and watch, since I was a new customer. He would tell me the possibilities for each cut and I'd tell him what I wanted.

Since I didn't have to worry about what came from where anymore, I decided to worry about a statement a friend had once made to me: She thought buying by the side was silly and uneconomical. "Why, there are cuts you'd never use, and you *have* to take it all, including fat and bone." I found out that at least part of this is nonsense. Whatever tough cuts one doesn't want whole can be ground into hamburger. The bones make excellent soup, and, as for the fat, not only is it wise to make friends with the birds (and they *really* appreciate suet during the winter), but there are directions on the cans of lye one can buy in the store for making perfectly good soap. (I will only add to these directions: make sure and keep boric acid in the house in case of burns if you are handling lye, and for goodness sakes, wear goggles!) But the real argument in my case was my knowledge of me. I knew that if I bought only supermarket sales, I'd never have the courage to buy sirloin or porterhouse steaks, so we'd end up with little else than chopped meat and chuck. Buying by the side I'd get a full range of goodies with only one shopping trip as well.

When I arrived at the butcher's he brought out half a beef carcass, hung it up on his beam scale, and totaled 325 pounds. Then he cut out the inner fat. (This is the best quality fat on the beef; it is the suet, the fat you use for cooking and candlemaking. The outer fat is softer and spongier and good for little else than soap.) I had told the butcher I wanted all the fat and bones, so he set up a box for these. He asked me if I wanted the kidney, and I told him I certainly did! One of the things my mother cooks extremely well is kidney stew, and I keep up the tradition.

The next thing he did was to cut the side into quarters, and the quarters into two pieces. Then came the questions. He told me the possibilities for each cut. I chose among them, and he carved accordingly. For instance, the sirloin could be made into steaks or roasts. I chose steaks, since my family is small. The boneless sirloin tips could be made into steaks or roasts. I chose a combination. I had him cut the round into roasts, reserving a few slices for round steaks. I like to stew the short ribs, so he cut those into pieces. If I hadn't liked short ribs, I could have had the meat cut off and added to the hamburger. (The hamburger, by the way, is made up of the toughest meat, and the bits and scraps cut away from the bones and the choicer portions.)

He asked me if I wanted stew beef reserved from the hamburger. The first time I had him take out a few pounds, but the hamburger turned out to be too fatty. (He sells "choice" grade meat, which is *by definition* fatty.) So after that time I didn't reserve stew beef, but stewed short ribs, chuck steaks, and occasionally the bottom round instead. Another way to achieve less fatty hamburger is to have a beef heart ground into it. (The beef heart doesn't come with the side; you have to ask for it separately. Its price per pound is a lot cheaper than for the side, and there is almost no waste to it.) I always ask that the hamburger be ground twice so it is well mixed.

We love corned beef, and my butcher keeps an excellent brine going, so, at no extra charge, he cut off the brisket and

tagged it with our name, put it in his brine barrel and told
me to come and get it in two weeks.

Freezing raw meat is simple. I merely wrap it in freezer
paper (shiny side in) in as airtight a fashion as possible, or put
it in freezer containers when I have appropriately shaped
ones, label and date it and put it on the quick-freeze shelf of
the freezer (if there is one) or I place it near the walls of our
chest-style freezer. *Don't* pile it in the middle of the freezer
—it takes *much* longer to freeze that way. You are warned.

It takes just as long to wrap as it does to cut up a side of
beef, so I've gotten into the habit of pitching in and doing the
wrapping and labeling and dating as the butcher cuts up the
meat. Dating is important, since you don't want to "lose" a
sirloin steak for a few years!

Bone (or have boned) everything you can—it saves space
and fuel, and makes for good soups.

Pack meat in the quantities in which you will be using
it. If two generally eat, don't put ten hamburgers in one
package unless you plan cold meat loaf for the next week.
Meat that has been frozen and thawed must be cooked
promptly, since it spoils quickly.

When you get home with a load of meat, load the hamburger into the freezer as fast as you can, especially in summer. Hamburger is the most perishable of all the cuts, and
can spoil very rapidly in hot weather. I pack mine in freezer
containers, with a piece of freezer paper between each hamburger so that they can be lifted out individually.

Usually, I ask the butcher for some tail bones (commonly
called ox tails). They are delicious for soups, stews, and chili
con carne. He frequently throws them in as a bonus. I have
him score them for me, so I can cut them up at home and put
them in freezer containers—one tail has a lot of meat on it,
too much for a single meal for us, in fact.

My butcher is a master at the art of sausage making, so

I also make sure to find out what kinds of sausages and cold cuts he has been putting up recently and buy five or ten pounds of each. We particularly like a veal sausage called bratwurst, which seems to have caraway and chives as flavorings, and is out of this world! Find out if your butcher makes it. I buy whole salamis and liverwursts from him at half the supermarket price, then I cut them into chunks at home and freeze them in small plastic bags.

For a long time I shied away from buying veal by the side. Of course the result was that we never had veal. Then once, when I couldn't seem to get any beef, I ordered a side of veal and discovered that although veal sounds expensive ($1.50 per pound by the side as against 80¢ per pound for beef at that point), it isn't all that expensive after all. There is very little waste on a side of veal—especially since there is almost no fat at all. Pork, on the other hand, is so *very* fatty that it is almost the same to buy it by the cut rather than the side. (By the way, my butcher sells wholesale either way—by the side or by the cut. I buy the side, Mel's mother has bought by the cut since Mel left home.)

Solid raw meats keep well frozen for at least a year. Ground meat and innards keep well for at least five months (after a while the fat in the ground meat gets a little pasty. It is not harmful, just not particularly tasty.)

Remember all that fat? When we get home I chop it into small cubes and boil it in an enormous kettle of water. When most of the fat has been rendered out, I strain it, let it harden and pick it off the water it was boiled in. (When cooking down fat watch to see it is still steaming—in other words, don't let the water all boil away. There is a technique of rendering fat without water, but it requires careful watching. If the fat gets too hot it can burst into flame. Rendering it in water keeps it below that critical point. I find that if I skim off the hardened fat and boil it up once more in clear water, let that harden and skim it off, I can melt it and pour it into a plastic bucket and have it keep for months without going rancid. This is the equivalent to two washings in water: it gets out the trace blood and impurities which might make it go bad. Then we can make soap out of it at our leisure.

Then there are the bones. This is what I do with them.

BEEF BONE SOUP

Bones from a side or quarter of beef
Water or vegetable stock

I put the bones in the basket of my canner, until it is two-thirds full. Then I put water or vegetable stock up to the two-thirds mark, bring the canner up to fifteen pounds pressure for forty-five minutes, and let the pressure go down of its own accord. Then I lift out the basket of bones, discard them and put in more bones (but no more water). I repeat this again and again until all the bones and meat traces are used up. Then I strain the soup concentrate, cool it until the fat hardens, discard the fat (or wash it and add it to the soap bucket), and freeze the soup in ice cube trays (or can it, whichever seems more convenient).

Notice that I do *not* use salt. It is very difficult to gauge how much to put in since I am making concentrate. I always salt the stock when I use it. This has the additional advantage of my being able to serve it to people on salt-restricted diets.

Follow the same recipe for any kind of bones—they all make good soup, but with different flavors. I use pork bones, veal bones, turkey bones, chicken bones, whatever turns up.

Freezing Vegetables

I said that the main space of my freezer goes for meat. But I do freeze a decent supply of vegetables as well.

Most vegetables require blanching before freezing. A few do best if cooked through. Freezing will stop any bacterial action in frozen food, but will merely slow down the enzymic action, which gradually changes the color, texture and food value of fresh vegetables. In order to destroy those enzymes, we simply dip the cleaned, prepared vegetables in boiling water for a given number of minutes (how long varies from vegetable to vegetable), drain, cool as rapidly as possible (so they don't overcook and become mushy) and pack them. The cooling time should be twice the cooking time, and should be done by dousing the blanching basket in ice water. Reuse the blanching water to save time and fuel. The water picks up some of the juices from the vegetables, so you might decide to use separate waters for different foods. If you are not going to use separate waters for different foods, you might want to leave broccoli, Brussels sprouts, and other strong tasting foods for last. On the other hand, if you are going to freeze mushrooms, you might want to use the mushroom water for blanching peas, or other foods that might profit from the mushroom taste. Use your judgment and imagination.

The first time you freeze vegetables, do one batch from beginning to end to get the hang of it. Once you've done it you'll find you can work two blanchers alternately if you are clever about it.

Prepare (pick, wash well and cut up) all the vegetables you are going to use in one freezing session. (Be reasonable about quantities—you want your vegetables to be *fresh*.) Set your covered kettles of water to boil. Don't overfill; remember the vegetables will displace water. The general rule is, use a gallon of water to a quart of vegetables. Get together all the freezer containers you will need, and fill two dishpans with ice water. Put a batch of food to be blanched into a blanching colander, immerse it in the boiling water, wait for it to boil again, then set your timer for the appropriate number of minutes. When your timer goes off, *immediately* remove the vegetables, drain for a moment, run cold water over the vegetables and immerse the whole thing in a dishpan of ice water. When it is partly cooled (say for as long as the vegetables were blanched), pack the vegetables into freezer containers (leaving a half-inch head room: vegetables containing water expand when they freeze).

As each freezer container is packed, cover it and put it immediately into the second dishpan of ice water. As the ice in the dishpans melts, add more. Once the total cooling time has been twice the blanching time, label and date your containers and into the freezer they go. (You might want to open the containers a crack and drain out any excess water before freezing. Some people actually drain the cooled vegetables loose on a towel laid over a screen.) The key to the process is being very precise about the blanching time. There is, however, one rub, or at least so I have found.

Some authorities recommend that the timing be counted from when the vegetables are first immersed in the actively boiling water. Others say count the time from when the water returns to an active boil. The only problem is, some stoves are hotter than others. City gas is hotter, and therefore returns a pot to a boil faster than my propane gas stove. In fact, my mother-in-law's propane fueled stove is faster than mine; it is run off a much larger tank, which might have something to do with it. I did some canning on a neighbor's electric stove, and that is faster even than city gas. If we get a good hot wood fire going in our wood stove, that seems faster yet. I suspect this is why the difference in instructions from instruction book to instruction book. So I suggest that you determine your method by experimentation.

The manual that comes with your freezer will give a blanching time chart. It is best to use this as a jumping off point for experimentation. In any case, blanching times will range between one minute (for greens and chopped vegetables) to five minutes for stuff like green soy beans and large Brussels sprouts. All vegetables should be sorted for size since big ones will require more time to heat through than the small ones.

I would like to remark, however, that *if* you are cooking with propane gas, and want to start your timing from the time you put the stuff in rather than the time it returns to a boil, use more than the recommended gallon of water per quart of vegetables; or do fewer vegetables at one time. This way the vegetables will not cool down the water so drastically. Ideally, you should use proportions of vegetable to water small enough so you can add the vegetables without reducing the water temperature to under a boil. In any case, the idea is to blanch the vegetables until they are heated through, *but no longer.* Freezing tenderizes vegetables. If they are blanched too long and then frozen, they become mush. Experiment a bit and see what's appropriate to your stove. Once you've determined the proper method, be precise about the blanching time, and keep records!

Any vegetable may be frozen as a purée for baby or invalid food, or just because you like it that way. Cook it as you usually do, purée it, and return to a boil to remove air. Cool as rapidly as possible, pack, and freeze. And for baby food freeze those purées in ice cube trays. Thaw out a couple of cubes at a time as needed.

If you have trouble with vegetables not keeping good color, try adding a splash of lemon either to the blanching water or the cooling water. This works especially well with cauliflower.

It is most efficient to have two people work at freezing vegetables—one preparing the food for blanching, and perhaps packing it when partly cooled, the other taking care of the blanching and first cooling. But if you are working by yourself, you will quickly get a feeling for how fast you can go, and will start the next batch to boil either just before your timer goes off, or when you have accomplished enough of the cooling process of what's gone before to keep working constantly but in an unhurried fashion. Don't get frantic—just work effectively and efficiently.

There has been a lot of discussion among health food types about the evils of blanching in boiling water. One neighbor complained to us about the quality of some vegetables she had steam-blanched and frozen. "They were mushy and tough at the same time!"

I told her that the quality of her vegetables depended on their being heated through as fast as possible. What had probably happened was that the outside had been cooked by the steam while the inside stayed cold. The pitch of her voice rose. "All those vitamins lost in that boiling water!" she exclaimed. "Why, the water actually changes color!"

I shrugged. The time necessary for steam blanching is about twice the time the boiling method requires. I knew from experience that the vegetables lose juices either way. If that sort of thing worried her, I told her, then she had a choice. Either she could gather her organically grown vegetables, process them within two hours of picking, when at their peak, or she could go to the supermarket during the winter and buy "fresh" vegetables. I myself wasn't convinced that the boiling-water blanched produce was any more deficient than the supermarket produce, which of necessity languishes in cold storage, is shipped, delayed, handled, and packed into plastic containers. And they are certainly not organically grown. Either way some of the nutritional value is lost. I will stick by my boiling-water blanching technique and enjoy attractive, good tasting products all winter.

In any case, when Mel and I have finished a freezing

session, *We don't throw away the blanching water.* We put it in a kettle with the bits and pieces of vegetables we'd put aside (the ends of string beans, the tough stalks from turnips and broccoli, the ends of asparagus and mushrooms, or whatever—even the pea pods) and we boil the whole business down. Within an hour or so we have a magnificent soup. We strain it, season it and have some for dinner. Then we pack the remainder into freezer containers for exquisite lunches and dinners we would quite literally have poured down the drain.

Freezing Fruits

Freezing fruit is easy. Berries we just put into freezer containers, label and date and stick in the freezer. They may be rolled in dry sugar if you like, or may be frozen in a sugar water syrup (see below). Other fruits (except apples, which we store fresh and don't freeze) may be peeled and cored and sliced, put into freezer containers and covered with a cold sugar or honey syrup. (I learned from my mother-in-law to make the syrup to taste. The books invariably say to use far heavier syrups than either she or I like.) I am told that apple slices require blanching for three minutes before freezing or else they get mealy. Fruits and fruit juices keep well at least a year.

Freezing Other Foods

Butter freezes very well, and will keep at least six months. I hear salt butter freezes better than sweet butter, but I've never had trouble with either. Baked goods (or partly baked goods, or dough) must be wrapped in tin foil, freezer paper or plastic bags in an air-tight fashion and put in the freezer. Be sure and date them. Fully cooked baked goods will lose quality after four months, but last a little longer if frozen unbaked, say six months. Some people freeze bread dough when ready for its second rising.

We beat eggs and freeze them in ice cube trays, six eggs to the tray. If the chickens go on strike we always have an emergency ration. We also keep a freezer container for yolks and whites separately. If a recipe calls for an egg yoke, we put the leftover white in the freezer container devoted to whites, and mark each addition on the label. Whenever we want that number of egg whites, we have them ready to go. If you freeze eggs, either scramble them or separate them. Don't freeze them whole. The yolks will burst and bleed into the whites, and the shells will crack.

When I make dishes such as lasagna, or chili con carne, or some other long cooking dinner, I make enough to freeze up a batch in a freezer-to-oven container. Then when I don't feel like cooking I can just take a meal out of the freezer and pop it in the oven at 250° until it is heated through. Try not to use potatoes (they get mealy); sauces containing eggs like hollandaise or mayonnaise (they separate); lots of fat or oil (it gets rancid quickly when frozen). Try to use frozen cooked dinners within three months, while still at their peak.

In addition to the salamis and bolognas, and liverwursts I get from my butcher, I also slice and freeze leftover roast beef, corned beef, turkey, ham, meat loaf and pickled beef heart. These keep well for at least three months, and don't require cooking or heating when thawed. I frequently wrap them in foil so I can thaw them out quickly in a slow oven if unexpected company comes.

I also freeze cheese for cooking purposes—cheddar, mozarella, ricotta, cream cheese, cottage cheese. The texture is not as fine as that of cheese which has not been frozen, so it is not as useful for snacks as fresh.

Using Frozen Food

Frozen fruits may be thawed or served partly frozen very successfully. Frozen vegetables are best cooked frozen, or only thawed enough to separate the individual pieces. Since freezing tenderizes the vegetables, they require very little cooking time. They should be cooked in a very small amount of water (I use about a half cup to a quart of frozen vegetable). I make a habit of cooking down this liquid to serve as a sauce on the vegetable. This improves the flavor, not to mention the practice's nutritional benefits. Very tender vegetables like summer squash, I partly thaw so I can separate the pieces, then steam until it is just heated through. I find it holds its shape better handled this way.

By the way, while you are experimenting to find the best blanching times for vegetables, you might occasionally end up with frozen vegetables that are too soft. Don't despair. Be sure to correct your blanching time records, and serve the food as a purée or en casserole. Frozen puréed vegetables take a devil of a time to get from the brick stage to a mush, so I've taken to partly thawing them in the refrigerator for an hour before I plan to cook them. Then I heat them in a double boiler. If you cook them frozen solid in a kettle right over the fire, however, you must add a little—say, a quarter cup—water, because the bottom might burn before it thaws enough to make moisture.

Puréed baby food cubes I thaw in a custard cup set in a pan of simmering water. This does very nicely indeed. Don't hold it over for another meal, however, unless you have brought it to a full boil. Either eat it yourself, or add it to the soup or stewpot or something. Frozen foods should not be allowed to sit uncooked for any length of time because they go bad very quickly.

I am in the habit of taking frozen meats out of the freezer in the morning and setting them on a plate on top of the refrigerator to thaw. But I keep my house pretty cool, so you might find you are better off thawing meat in the refrigerator. Count on five hours per pound for roasts, less for steaks and chops. Meat may be cooked frozen, too, but tends to come out dryer that way. Obviously cooking time will be much longer if meat starts out frozen—count on between ten minutes to half an hour per pound more. If you want to thaw out meat fast, put it in a waterproof container and set it in cold *(not hot)* water. Change the water periodically. (If you set it in hot water, the outer layer might thaw and spoil before the inside thaws out.) As soon as any frozen raw meat is thawed, cook it or else it will spoil. My own experience is that frozen smoked food, like bacon, does not require immediate cooking upon thawing. But I freeze it in quantities that will be used within a couple of days anyway.

At first you will have to adapt your cooking techniques to the products you are freezing. But pretty soon you will be able to adapt the products to your favorite cooking techniques. So don't get discouraged if you don't achieve perfection at first. Who knows, you might come up with something terrific by accident!

Postscript

Even if you don't have a freezer, don't despair. Freezing as a food preservation technique is not particularly new. In the good old days, the proverbial mama used to make up a whole batch of pies at a time in midwinter, and set them out in a shed somewhere. There they would freeze solid, and she could bring them in and bake them as she needed them. Meat, too, was kept frozen in very cold weather in "meat safes" (screened-in boxes)—perhaps not for quite as long as in the present day thermostatically controlled home freezer.

As Mel puts it, "There's a reason why the traditional time for slaughtering was in late fall." In the days of home canning of meat, that cellar under the farmhouse that had none of the modern conveniences was as nice and cold in late autumn as a butcher's cold storage room is today. There's no way you can put up a whole cow in cans in one day, so you can be sure the cold cellar was put to good use! Indeed, Mel's mother tells me that she thinks her easy labor and delivery of Mel was due in part to putting up meat for the winter! He was born in January, right after a slaughtering session. She put up all her own meat in those days, so there was little need for her to do deep knee bends and back flexes to get *her* muscles in tone!

CHAPTER 9

DRYING FOOD

Greer speaking

My first experience with drying food came about accidentally. When I lived in the city I would buy fresh dill weed whenever it was available and I would use it as long as it lasted. When it was gone I would miss it sorely. But once when I was in a hurry, I just stuck the paper bag full of dill into the refrigerator and forgot about it for a couple of weeks. Then I found it. Before tossing it out, I looked into the bag. Instead of rotting, as it would have done in a plastic bag, it had dried out nicely. It was still bright green in color, and when I rubbed them the fine leaves powdered and gave off that lovely dill aroma. So I rubbed them off the stems, added the stems to a soup I was cooking up, and packed the leaves in a jar to use when my green grocer failed me.

We don't dry much of our food, but we do dry some, though I use more traditional methods now. I'll explain what we do, and describe other methods briefly. In the bibliography at the end of the book I'll give sources for more details on these methods.

A Dark, Dry Place

I dry my herbs by tying them in small bunches and hanging them, head down, from a line tied across our attic. The idea is to have a dry, dark place. Once I hung some herbs in an unused room with windows. The herbs dried well enough, but they also bleached and lost their flavor entirely. The sunlight did that. So if you don't have a dark attic, and your basement's too damp, try the back of a mothball-free closet. If the place is apt to be dusty, shape a funnel of paper and use it as a dust jacket to hang over the top of the herb bunches. *Don't* use plastic because the moisture won't be able to escape and the herbs will rot instead of drying.

The best time to pick herbs for drying is when the plant is budding for flowering. The flavor is at its peak then. Leave the buds on, but remove any damaged leaves. If you don't manage to start your drying at exactly the right time, however, don't despair. Starting late is better than never. The result will still be better than purchased dried herbs.

I should mention that there is some controversy in the literature about whether or not to wash green herbs before drying them. I tried it but don't like it. So I pick them the day after a light rain, when the dew has dried off. I make sure to pick off any dirty-looking leaves. If you decide to wash your green herbs before drying them, rinse them under a gentle spray of water, shake off all the water you can, then spread them on a clean towel for a while before proceeding with whatever technique you've chosen.

If it is the seeds you are after, like dill seed or carrot seed or coriander, rub the seeds off the plant when they look dry and mature, spread them out on a cloth or paper in a dark, dry place for a few days before storing them. Or you can pick the flowerheads with a bit of stem and hang them up in bunches, as for green herbs. But be careful if you do this— the seeds are apt to fall off when they are near ready, just like in the great outdoors. Even if the seeds look and feel dry when you first gather them, there will be some moisture in them just from being outside. If you pack them right away, they will mold. If it is seeds you are after, don't wash them before giving them their final indoor drying.

My neighbor told us you can dry your mature shell beans and peas this way. Let the pods mature on the vines, then when there is danger of frost pull the vines, tie in bunches, and hang in a dark, dry place until the vines have dried out and the pods have "papered" over (dried out). Put them in a big burlap sack and beat the sack with a broom or stick. Then make a bean-or-pea-sized hole in the bottom of the bag and pour out the shelled beans or peas. Pick over, removing damaged or unsightly ones, "pasteurize" them in a 250° oven for thirty minutes (shaking them frequently), then store them away in a light-and-air-proof container. This pasteurization kills bugs, molds, etc., that might make the beans spoil.

If I don't have many mature bean pods, I spread them on a paper in the attic until they've dried quite thoroughly. They shouldn't be allowed to touch each other, or they will mold. Then I shell and proceed as before.

Freshly gathered nuts (like butternuts and walnuts) really should be spread out in the sun for a few days until the outer rinds dry up (but bring them in before evening so the dew doesn't affect them). Carrying them in and out seems like too much bother to me, so I spread them on a screen in the attic. If they show a tendency to mold (as they might if allowed to touch each other, especially if weather is damp), I put them in a 250° oven for half an hour, then proceed as before. When the outer rind is crinkly and completely dry, they may be put into a sack in a cool place, or shelled and stored in the freezer. By the way, butternuts have a divine flavor, but are (or so I thought) impossible to crack neatly. Then Mel's father showed me how to put them in a vise, and tighten it slowly until the nut just cracks, holding it with one hand so it doesn't shatter. So don't throw away the nuts from your trees, as one family I know did, because they couldn't seem to get at the meat.

Pan Drying

I've never pan-dried herbs, but a friend does all her catnip that way. She told me that she strips the leaves off the stems and puts them in an ungreased frying pan over the lowest fire she can manage. She makes sure to shake the leaves around in the pan from time to time to prevent scorching until they are completely dry (crumble when rubbed). Her cat seems to relish the result. She says it doesn't take long—maybe half an hour.

I do pan-dry my squash seed and pumpkin seed (for eating, not planting). Wash the seeds and spread on muslin or a couple of layers of paper towels in a dry, dark place for a week or so. Then spread on a cookie tin in a 200° oven for half an hour, pack them away in an envelope or a jar, and when you want to use them pan-toast, butter and salt them. The seeds from the smaller winter squashes like acorn squash are tastiest.

To dry seeds for planting, *omit the oven-drying step;* be sure to label them so you know what you're planting.

Oven Drying

Our first year here, when I was winding up my garden, I found I had only a few things left from our summer of good eating. There were a handful of carrots, some very tiny kale plants, which I had started too late to have them come to much; swiss chard, which was still sending up a few greens here and there, and the greens from a very short row of turnips. Not to mention four or five onions. Somehow I felt we wouldn't survive the winter if I didn't manage to preserve in some way those few carrots, onions, kale, turnip greens and chard. So I decided to try a dried vegetable mixture for soups.

I figured the greens would dry most quickly, so I did them first. I stripped the leaves from the coarse inner stems, since the stems would take a longer time to dry than the thin leaves would. Then I sliced the leaves up fine, (the size doesn't matter, but the uniformity does) and spread them on aluminum cookie sheets. I set my oven for 150°, put three cookie sheets of greens inside, and propped the oven door a little open with the handle of a wooden spoon. Every half hour or so, I glanced in the oven to see what was happening, and shook the tins and stirred the greens around a bit so they wouldn't stick. After an hour they looked quite dry. I picked out a leaf and rubbed it. It crumbled. I spied a leaf which had a bit of stem in it, and tried breaking the stem. It was too supple for safety, so I let them go another half hour. When I tested again the stems broke, so I knew that they were completely dry. They really need watching, especially toward the end. I packed the greens into a coffee can with a plastic lid and stored it away.

Next day I decided to do the onions. I chopped them until the pieces were uniform in size. (The size doesn't matter, but the uniformity does. I chose pieces a quarter the size of my little finger nail. The smaller they are the faster they'll dry.) I spread them one layer deep on my aluminum cookie tins and gave them the same treatment. They took four or five hours. Also, they seemed to be drying unevenly, so I switched them around from time to time, put the bottom one on top (etc.). I knew they were dry when they got brittle. I packed these away. The third day I did the same thing to the carrots. I have a nice clamp-on vegetable grater-slicer-dicer contraption. It has a number of different blades for different effects—one slices, one grates, one makes tiny julienne sticks. I happened to choose the tiny julienne sticks. I put my scrubbed, peeled carrots through the vegetable grater, spread them out one layer deep in the cookie tins and popped them in the oven. These took about eight hours. Since I watched conscientiously and shifted the trays around periodically I managed to get them nicely dry without scorching them. They really need watching, especially toward the end!

All in all, I did two large coffee cans full of dried vegetables . . . different kinds of greens, onions, carrots. And I used them happily all winter long.

If I wanted a cup of soup, I thawed out a few cubes of frozen soup stock, or used boullion cubes. I added water, put in a couple of tablespoons of dried vegetables and boiled it for about five minutes. That's all there was to it. And I discovered that the dried vegetable mixture was delicious in cheese dips. We liked our dried vegetable mixture so much that this year we've tripled our supply.

I follow the same drying procedure when I have citrus rind or fresh coconut.

When we finally got our Franklin stove working, I discovered I could dry food very conveniently by chopping it into uniform, small pieces and spreading it on a lightly oiled aluminum cookie sheet, and setting it on top of the stove. If I stir it around every once in a while and turn the sheet, the food dries very evenly. If it seems to be drying too quickly, I shift it to a cooler part of the stove top. It still takes a long time (orange peel, for instance, takes about three hours when we have a good fire going), but somehow it doesn't seem like work.

A Warm, Cozy Kitchen

In the old days of wood cookstoves, which did the double role of cooking and heating, when the kitchen was hot, and I mean hot, since the meat was tough and needed hours and hours of boiling and roasting, and breads and pies needed baking, and beer needed brewing, and flat irons for ironing clothing had to be heated on that same stove, other drying techniques were used. A screened-in box with wooden slatted shelves was hung over the wood cookstove, which was kept going almost constantly in the flurry of other activities. Food to be dried was placed on the trays and left there; the trays were shifted around periodically to allow even drying. Some goods, such as mushrooms and string beans, were put on strings and hung behind the stove to dry.

For more details, on these methods, see *The Foxfire Book.*

CHAPTER 10
ROOT CELLARING

Greer speaking

If you live in an old house you will always be a little bit behind. This and that comes up comes up and plans are somehow left behind. Everything gets done sooner or later, usually later—but it does get done. Or so I keep telling myself by way of comfort.

"Mel," I complained well into the autumn of our first year here.

"Hm." He was reading *TV Guide* that time.

"We've *got* to make that root cellar."

"We will," was the comforting reply.

Another week went by.

"Melvin Fitting, my apples will freeze in that shed, and so will everything else. And the upstairs is beginning to smell like onions! I've *got* to have that root cellar!" I paused for a moment. Mel wasn't there at all. Half an hour later he appeared in the kitchen and asked for "that old army blanket you got from my father." I located the blanket and he disap-

163

peared with it down the cellar stairs. A few minutes later he
called up from the depths, "Okay, here's your root cellar." I
went down and looked. Gone were my visions of a nice neat
root cellar with shelves and racks and little compartments.
"Oh, my," I said.

Along the front wall of our cellar was a sort of rock-lined
alcove which had once been a stairway to an outside en-
trance on the porch. This porch had been cemented over and
the doorway sealed up. In the process a good deal of rubble
had fallen into the old stairwell. Mel had stirred this rubble
around a bit, making it sort of flat, then he had set up boards
on some rocks. The effect was not beautiful. The army blanket Mel had tacked up as a door was not beautiful either, but
he seemed pleased.

"Now what we need is a couple of trash burners," Mel
said in a satisfied tone.

"A couple of what?"

"Trash burners. Garbage cans with holes in them that
people burn trash in. Just what you need for the onions and
stuff."

"All right, let's go and get the trash burners," I said. We
also got 100 pounds of potatoes and 150 pounds of onions to
put in them. And squash. And pumpkins. And later, apples
and carrots, and the cabbage from our garden. And you
know, it all kept well. Clear through to spring, much of it. So
it wasn't a beautiful root cellar. But it worked. Someday
when we get the time we'll build a lavish one. Until then
we'll eat well anyway.

**Sorting Vegetables and Fruits
for Root Cellar Storage**

One doesn't simply dump potatoes in a root cellar. Some
potatoes are better "keepers" than others. Some are healthy,

some are bruised. Potatoes must be sorted. Only store the best. Eat the worst right away. Same goes for onions, apples, anything, in fact. Our first sorting session was nerve-racking. I had no experience to go on, so I did it by instinct, and never quite believed it would work. It did, though, so I gained confidence. After a couple of years of successful root-cellaring, now even I can describe to someone else my criteria for a good "keeper."

First some general principles, then I'll talk about each item separately.

A vegetable or fruit will *not* keep well if it is in any way damaged, if it was unhealthy to begin with, or if it has been treated roughly. In general, very minute or gigantic, oversized specimens will not keep as well as a medium-sized one. Now to specifics.

ONIONS: Some authorities say that onions grown from sets don't keep well. But I've been assured by various gardeners around here that they don't find this to be the case if they are careful about sorting. (Sometimes the seed stalk grows right out of the center of the onions and doesn't flatten out when it drys up, so there is an air hole down into the middle of the onion. These don't keep well.) In any case, if you've grown onions, whether from set or from seeds, they must be dried out before storing. If the weather is good, do this by merely pulling the onion out of the ground and letting it lie on the ground in the garden for a few days until the skin has "papered over" (got that nice dry shiny look), and the greens and the little roots are completely dried up. Or you can just lay them one layer deep on old refrigerator or dishwasher racks and set them in the shed or in the attic to dry. When they are thoroughly dried they can be sorted and packed.

I reject for storage any onions that show signs of growing. I reject those which have flattish "necks," that is, the part where the greens grow out. I also reject any onion that has a long spongy neck, for they are the first to go soft. I reject those onions that have scars or bruises into the flesh of the onion (cracks in the skin don't matter), or those that are missing most of their skin. The rejects are packed separately and used first, the others stored in our trash burners. Net bags or bushel baskets are also satisfactory. The idea is that air should be allowed to circulate through them. If possible, for storage purposes always plant onion varieties that are recognized as "good keepers" (ask your seed salesman).

POTATOES: Like onions, potatoes must be dried a bit before storage. Either let them lie in the field for a couple of days after digging, or if the weather is freezing, put them in baskets in a shed somewhere out of the light for a week. Then sort and store. Late potatoes (harvested in autumn) keep better than early potatoes (those harvested during summer), so if you are planning potatoes for winter, do a planting that will be ready in the fall. Around here a mid-June planting gives ample time for late potatoes to mature. Ask your gardening neighbors what's the story for your climate. We store these, too, in trash burners. Other possibilities are bushel baskets, or bags with ventilation holes, or burlap bags. Separate for immediate use any potatoes that have cuts or bruises, and the very tiny ones, or any that seem soft. Potatoes, like anything else you wish to store for a long period, should be handled carefully. *Put them, don't drop them* into their storage containers. Don't toss them around. This is important. Our potatoes keep well into spring. Toward the end they may start growing, so we plant those sprouters that are left in June.

ROOT VEGETABLES: Carrots, beets, white winter radishes, parsnips, salsify, turnips—they should all be allowed to rest in the field for half a day before packing for storage. Authorities say this is for the purpose of getting the "field heat" out of them. I take this to mean it gives the root a chance to go dormant. In any case, I pack carrots, beets and white winter radishes and turnips in dirt. The authorities say use sand, but I didn't have any when I needed it, and my neighbors tell me that dirt does just as well. They're right, it does. I stole it from a pile of top soil we never got spread around the lawn. As the vegetables get eaten I'll use the dirt for starting sets for the garden in the spring. I thought I was being very clever by collecting (and asking my father-in-law to collect) old dresser drawers to pack them in. Now the dovetails of the drawers are pulling apart from the damp and —well, you can imagine the mess. Plastic pails seem to be the best containers after all, or at least my turnips think so.

The way root vegetables are packed is simple. Remember, they are roots. First I put a layer of dirt on the bottom of the containers. Then I put a layer of carrots (or whatever) making sure that they lay on their side without touching one another. By the way, I cut off all but a half inch of the greens before I pack them. That little bit of greens left on the crown keep the vegetable from "bleeding." I cover it with dirt, put another layer of carrots, and so on until the container is filled up. The top layer is dirt. Of course I set aside for immediate use any damaged ones, softish ones, and very tiny ones. I use separate containers for different vegetables as far as possible.

We were running out of space in the root cellar, so when the time came for fall plowing and the parsnips and salsify had to be brought in, I used another style of packing for root-cellar storage. I cut off their greens, leaving a half inch of stems, and put them in plastic bags like those that celery and carrots come in—with ventilating holes. I've found it is not enough just to poke a slit in a regular plastic bag with a knife. These close up and don't allow the vegetables to "breathe." Actual holes must be cut or punched. About twelve little holes to a bag is about right—holes the size of loose-leaf paper holes. And the bag should be packed full.

Toward spring the vegetables might begin sprouting a bit, but this does no harm. Our gourmet chickens get the sprouts, while we eat the roots.

WINTER SALAD makings, like escarole, chinese cabbage, celery and fennel, store pretty well for at least a month. Pack them in ventilated plastic bags.

APPLES: We stored our apples in bushel baskets last year. There are "good keepers" and "bad keepers" among apples, too. I store Spies, Romes and Ida Reds. Greenings are also said to keep well.

Windfalls are apples that are fully ripe and have fallen off the tree of their own accord. They won't keep very long. We always get a basket of windfalls for immediate use, but *pick* the apples we will store for winter use. This means the apples are slightly underripe; picked, they will not be damaged by a drop from the tree. Which means: *Don't shake the tree to get them down.* They'll fall and bruise and the bruise will start to rot, and there go your apples.

I sort apples into three containers. One is for perfect apples which *retain a bit of stem.* These are the long keepers. I don't cheat, either. If an apple looks at all dented or bruised, I pack it separately. The second box is for perfect apples which don't have stems. These do *not* keep as long as the perfect ones. They are my second longest keepers. The third box I put in front of the root cellar for immediate use. These are the apples with flaws and blemishes: a bruise, a worm hole, a cut in the skin, funny looking scabs on the skin, or whatever. Any apple I have doubts about goes into this third box for use as soon as I've used up the windfalls, or for applesauce.

Some people wrap each piece of fruit in soft paper. I don't do this because it is hard to look them over. But try some both ways and see which suits you.

LATE CABBAGE keeps better than early cabbage, so

plan your plantings so that the heads you want to store are firming up when cold weather arrives. Store them as long as you can in the garden, then bring them in. (Plant varieties that are known to be "good keepers.") What you want to avoid is their freezing solid, thawing out and freezing again; but that's a rule for anything to be stored fresh indoors. Purple cabbage stores beautifully, as does green winter cabbage. Savoy cabbage (the crinkly kind) doesn't keep very well for long, so use it within a month. I store my cabbage in the root cellar, in wooden crates or bushel baskets. I place them head down. Some people store them upside down with their roots still attached, but Mel's father warned me they might dry out that way.

My cabbages kept beautifully last year. We ate the last one at the end of February. I must admit, though, that the outer leaves of that very last cabbage had begun to mold. But when I tore those off a sound crisp cabbage appeared inside and we were satisfied. Once picked, the cabbages *must be kept cool.*

The ideal temperature for storing all these things is just above freezing: 35–40° does nicely. Our root cellar stays an even 40° all winter long, once cold weather sets in.

Some things require a slightly higher temperature for good storage. Green tomatoes will ripen up gradually if kept at 50°. They do so unevenly, so they must be sorted over every couple of days or so. We had tomatoes for Thanksgiving last year, and this year ran out only a matter of a week before Thanksgiving. I've known people who keep tomatoes until Christmas.

I like to spread the green tomatoes one layer deep in cardboard boxes. It makes them easy to look over. Some people store them without stems, which has the advantage that the stem on one tomato doesn't poke holes in the others. Other people store their tomatoes with stems: the advantage of this is that if you spread a damp cloth over them once or twice a week the stems hold the cloth at a proper height and the tomatoes don't dry out and get crinkly.

Squash and pumpkins want a slightly higher temperature for storage, too. It is best if you can spread them out without their touching each other, but stack them (gently) if you must. Look over them periodically to see that no spots of rot are starting. If you do see a spot, use the squash immediately. Or if it is too big, use what you need for a meal or two, then freeze the rest as a purée. I find winter squash keeps better than pumpkins.

Since these things do well at about 50°, which, it just so happens, is the temperature of the main part of our cellar, that's where we put them. Squash especially should be stored in the dark, or else they will "rust" (they turn color and get stringy).

But the Apples Smell Like Cabbage!

I've read all sorts of warnings about not packing apples and cabbages together. It seems potatoes pick up odors of the sort that turnips give out. I have only one root cellar, so I can't get fancy about keeping things separate. The first year I just hoped for the best.

What I discovered is that while it is probably a good idea to pack fruits and vegetables separately, and to put strong smelling ones away from the less odoriferous ones, it is not crucial. I found that as long as the contents of the root cellar are in good health, they don't smell. If I begin to smell onions, I know that there is an onion rotting somewhere. So I dig it out and remove it. Or if I smell apples, there's an apple rotting somewhere, so I search it out. And my root cellar just doesn't smell; nor do my apples smell like cabbages or turnips.

A few more remarks. If your root cellar is apt to be dry, either sprinkle the floor with water periodically (if it's dirt) or put a pan of water on the floor somewhere, or put a box of sand down and keep that moist. Then the vegetables won't dry out. Our cellar is damp under any circumstances, so we don't have to think about it.

A root cellar should be ventilated. Since ours has a blanket as a door, we don't have to worry—enough air gets in around the edges of the blanket to keep the root cellar in good condition. If you are using a wood door, however, you might want to drill a few holes in it, and arrange a bit of wood or cardboard in such a way that you can cover them up or open them as you want to change either the temperature or the air circulation in the cellar storage area. If you can vent to outside, or to crawl space you might want to do that.

If you don't have a ready-made nook for a root cellar as we did, or if your cellar is too warm to use, there are other ways out. You can try using an unheated attic. Stick a thermometer up there and see what the temperature is at various times of the day in cold weather. If it is too cold, either leave the door open a crack, if that's possible, or put a well-shielded light bulb up there and leave it on. The vegetables have to be kept in the dark, though. Make arrangements accordingly. If it never gets *much* below freezing, it might be sufficient to just cover the vegetables with a blanket or some hay or something.

Some friends of Mel's parents moved out of a big old farmhouse with two cellars ideal for fresh vegetable storage into a little modern home with a heated basement. They weren't willing to give up the chance of storing food for winter, however, so they bought a second-hand refrigerator in working condition and put it in the basement. They pack it full of carrots and onions and other good things from their garden, adjust the temperature so it stays around 35°, and everything lasts beautifully throughout the winter.

Some vegetables may be stored in the garden. I haven't tried this, but the idea is to keep parsnips, salsify, carrots, celery and horseradish from freezing until the weather turns permanently cold (do this by mulching, or covering the rows with blankets). When the weather has turned, pull aside the mulch for a day or two and let the vegetables freeze, then put back the mulch. The mulch acts as insulation and keeps them from thawing during those occasionally warm days every winter turns out from time to time.

Sources of information on these techniques can be found in the books mentioned in the bibliography.

Fuzzy Little Friends

When I first set up the root cellar, I was determined not to set mousetraps. I didn't mind loosing an apple or two. But then one day I went down to fill the apple pail, and saw it wasn't a matter of an apple or two. Small bites had been taken out of each apple on the top of my four bushel baskets of apples. And mice droppings had duly dropped to those underneath. I had to do my sorting all over again, and I gave Mel my blessings as he set off to buy mousetraps. Yes, he had told me so. Since it was impossible to mouse-proof our dirt-floored, make-shift root cellar, it was the only way out. It still makes me sad. Tough luck, Greer, it's us or them.

Mel says, "Get the mice that come in in the fall. You won't have any trouble with more coming in after winter sets in." That's something you should pay attention to whether or not you have a root cellar. We set our mousetraps and caught five mice in one week; and then we were free of mice the rest of the winter.

Mel also says, "It seems a gory note on which to end the section." Tough luck, Mel, it's us or them.

CHAPTER 11

SIMPLE WINEMAKING

Melvin speaking

Nostalgia

When I was a teen-ager I used to mow lawns for money. One place I worked threw in a bonus, a recipe for dandelion wine (which I'll give later). I was at the age when I was just discovering drinking, and the prospect of a supply of something alcoholic that was so cheap was irresistible. So I made a gallon. My reactions were mixed. My friends felt the same about it. Still, it did the job, so to speak.

Years went by. I moved to the city, married, and moved back to the country. There were all these fields full of dandelion blossoms blowing in the sun. How could I resist? And once having begun again with dandelion wine, I was hooked. It was quickly followed by rose petal wine, clover wine, red raspberry wine, elderberry wine, blackberry wine, sumac wine, and that's just one summer. The future is wide open.

I've picked up quite a lot of information about home winemaking (and brewing) from the many excellent books on the market, and from my own experiments. It's astounding how often mathematics and chemistry get used. What I'll present in this chapter and the next is a compilation of what I've learned. I'm not giving recipes primarily (although there are some), rather I'm trying to give the principles on which recipes can be based. Then you can make up your own. I start with simple winemaking, then things get more and more complex. You can stop reading at whatever point you wish and still be able to make good wines. If you go on, you'll get more control over the finished product, so you'll probably make better wines.

One final word. Scattered through the chapter are lots of mathematical formulas, generally in English, though. They come up naturally, but if they give you too much trouble, ignore them. Instead of a formula for calculating how much sugar you'll need, you can work it out by trial and error. (It takes longer, though. The purpose of the math is to save time.)

Basic Basics

Yeast turns sugar into alcohol. This is the fundamental principle of winemaking and brewing. Everything else is simply technique designed to produce a tasty final product. Let's sketch the production of the simplest wine, sugar wine. It isn't very good by itself, but it can teach a lot about winemaking. And it is the basis of a whole family of flower wines. I'll say more about this later on.

Suppose we dissolve some ordinary white cane sugar in some water, then add some yeast, ordinary baker's yeast from the supermarket, say. The yeast will multiply in the solution, and after a day or two it will start producing alcohol. This is called *fermentation,* the solution is said to be *working.* A by-product of this working is carbon dioxide, a gas that escapes into the air (it's what you breathe out). The solution bubbles as the carbon dioxide escapes (it's also why soda bubbles). If you were making bread, the bubbles are what would make the bread rise. Eventually the process stops, the yeast dies and settles to the bottom as a sediment. The liquid now consists of water, alcohol, and possibly some sugar. Simple, isn't it?

I said fermentation eventually stops and the yeast dies. Why? This is important. There are two different reasons, depending. One is that the yeast cannot survive high alcohol concentration. Once the alcohol level reaches 10 to 15% or so (different with different yeasts) the yeast dies. It has committed suicide. This establishes an upper limit on wine strength, anything stronger must be made by removing some water from wine or beer, that is, by distilling, a complicated and illegal process. The second reason fermentation may stop is that the sugar is used up. Now, if I begin with a heavily sugared solution, the maximum alcohol level will be reached before all the sugar is used up. The process stops, and I have a sweet wine. If I start with only a little sugar, all of it will become alcohol and I will have a dry wine, though possibly less alcoholic than it might have been. So, the amount of sugar at the beginning is important in determining the eventual taste.

That's basically it. Now how do we ensure that what's supposed to happen happens? What can go wrong? Well, first, to dissolve the sugar, the water may have been heated. This is normal, and many wine recipes even call for some boiling. But yeast is killed by temperatures way short of boiling. So I wait until the solution has cooled below 80°F before adding the yeast (using a thermometer if really unsure).

Next, I mentioned baker's yeast. It is not the only kind

of yeast. There are thousands of them. The air is full of them. These air-borne yeasts are called wild yeasts. What they are varies from area to area. Traditional winemaking, say before Pasteur in the nineteenth century, used these wild yeasts, which is one reason wine taste varied from region to region. The difficulty is that some wild yeasts are not very nice (though some are fantastic). They produce alcohol, but they may also turn out by-products which don't have a good taste. Consequently, to be sure the work is done by the yeast I put in, the solution must be protected from air while it works. During the first few days of fermentation, the process is rather vigorous and much carbon dioxide is produced. This is heavier than air, so if the solution is in a crock or a kettle, with a lid or a plate over it—or, better yet, a plastic garbage bag tied over it—outside air has little chance of getting in. After a few days to a week, fermentation becomes less vigorous, less carbon dioxide is produced, so some air may seep in under the crock cover. Now the best thing I can do is to put the solution in a bottle and stopper it with a *fermentation lock*. This is a simple device that lets inside air out but doesn't let outside air in. They are generally plastic, cost a dollar or less, and are available from Sears, Ward's, and Macy's and winemakers' supply stores. Whatever you do, don't put the solution in a bottle and put the cap on tightly. The gas produced will build up and could burst the bottle, which is quite dangerous. Anyway, once in a bottle with a fermentation lock, the solution can be left for months with no danger.

The fear of wild yeasts is quite strong in some books on winemaking I've read. I suspect the problem, though real, is not great. Certainly many people make wine in open kettles using wild yeasts and succeed at it. I made the dandelion wine of my youth in an agate kettle with a loose cover, though now I use fermentation locks, but, also, now I generally leave the stuff to ferment and age in big bottles with fermentation locks for a year or so before final bottling. Many open-kettle winemakers are much more hasty.

To continue with possible problems, besides wild yeasts in the air there are also bacteria. (Bacteria are not the same as yeasts. They are both microscopic organism families, but quite different.) One widespread variety of bacteria can turn alcohol into vinegar. This is useful if vinegar is what you want, and is discussed later in the book. If it's alcohol you're after, covering and fermentation locks will take care of the problem. You see, vinegar bacteria need air to work, yeast doesn't.

One other problem, yeast has an ideal working temperature: it is different for different yeasts. For baker's yeast it is about 70°F. Much below this and fermentation will be very slow. Even colder and it will stop altogether, though the yeast will still be alive. Things will start going again if the temperature is raised. Much above this temperature and fermentation will be too fast for a good tasting result. Too hot, of course, and the yeast will die.

Well, that's about it, the basic theory of winemaking and some measures to ensure that theory and practice coincide. Now I'll summarize all this in recipe form, then in the next section I'll go through the making of a wine in more detail.

BASIC SUGAR WINE RECIPE

2 – 5 pounds sugar
1 gallon water
1 yeast packet

Boil water and stir in sugar. Use the following chart to determine sugar amount.

WINE TYPE	POUNDS OF SUGAR PER GALLON
dry	2 – 2 3/4
dividing line	3
slightly sweet	3 1/4 – 3 1/2
medium sweet	3 1/2 – 4
very sweet	4 – 5

Pour into a ceramic, uncracked crock or an *unchipped* agate kettle, cover, and let cool to 65° to 70°F. Stir in yeast, then tie a plastic bag tightly over the mouth of the crock or kettle. After five or six days, depending on how busy you are, siphon it into a gallon bottle and stopper it with a fermentation lock. Put any extra in a soda bottle and stopper that with cotton. Leave alone for three months. What happens next is covered in later sections.

Some comments. The above chart gives 3 pounds of sugar as the dividing line between sweet and dry. This means that some people find wine made with 3 pounds of sugar per gallon dry, some sweet. I find it has a trace of sweetness, not really enough to be called either sweet or dry. Personally I like a little more or a little less. That is, if I were trying for a sweet wine I'd use 3 1/4 to 3 1/2 pounds of sugar. If I were trying for a dry wine I'd use 2 3/4 pounds of sugar or less. Remember, the closer a dry wine is to two pounds, the less alcoholic it is (and a dry wine shouldn't be as alcoholic as possible, for best taste) and the closer a sweet wine is to 5 pounds, the sweeter it is. This dividing line between dry and sweet wine is the maximum alcoholic content possible, so most dry wines are less alcoholic than sweet wines.

If you want to use a large amount of sugar, four or five pounds per gallon, say, don't add it all at once, as it hurts the yeast action. Instead, add a few pounds at the start, the rest in a few days.

This recipe, like all other recipes in this chapter, can, of course, be doubled, or tripled, or whatever. You won't need extra yeast, however, for anything up to about five gallons of water. But don't worry about adding too much yeast; any extra simply settles out. Some people complain about a yeasty taste in homemade wines. The source isn't the use of too much yeast, generally it is due to bottling too soon.

Finally, remember the figures in the chart will vary in accuracy from person to person, with tastes and with winemaking techniques. Keep records and you'll quickly discover the right amounts for you. Use mine as a starting point.

The Days of Wine and Roses Stew

In the last section I sketched the making of sugar wine. Sugar wine, by itself, is not great fun to drink, though it is useful for spiking punch, or for drinking with added fruit syrups. But many interesting flower wines are nothing more than sugar wine with flowers added for part of the fermentation period to flavor it. In this section I'll describe, in great detail, the making of one such wine, rose petal wine.

The first thing needed is some sort of container like a crock in which the process can begin. The books call this a primary fermentor. It can be a crock, ceramic or glass, but not chipped or cracked, as bacteria stay in such places. It can be an agate kettle, again without chips. This is very important, wine can react with the metal if the agate is chipped. Or again it can be a plastic garbage can or wastebasket. These are probably easiest of all to handle. Or it can be an otherwise unusable crock or kettle with a polyethylene bag as liner. These, in appropriate sizes, are available from home winemaking supply stores quite cheaply. Whatever you use, make sure it is clean, and *rinsed*. All the books I've seen are pretty firm about not using aluminum kettles for fermentation (unless with a polyethylene liner). None of them are clear about why. There is some sort of belief that it is dangerous. This may be correct; I'd respect it.

I'll assume you have something suitable for a primary fermentor, at least one-half gallon bigger than the amount of wine you are making. I'll call it a crock, because that's what I use.

Now, we begin just as if we were making sugar wine. Let's say we want a slightly sweet wine, so we mix up 3 1/2 pounds of white cane sugar in one gallon of water. It is wise to bring the water to a boil to sterilize it, then, while it is hot, add the sugar. I don't always do it though. When it's cool enough to handle, I dump it into the crock. (Greer's note: "Rinse the crock with hot water before dumping in a hot solution or you may have another unusable crock!") Then it is covered with a plate or something, and it cools. When it is cool enough, and this may take overnight, the yeast can be added. The stuff is dumped into the crock, stirred up well, and the plate put back on. Or, probably better, we sometimes lay a plastic garbage bag across the mouth of the crock and tie it down with string. We leave the crock in a mildly warm place. Then we go away and smell roses.

Two days later we add 2 to 3 pints of rose petals to the concoction. Exactly how much depends on your taste. This you learn by experience. Then we let the thing work for another twelve days (two weeks from when we started). If it goes an extra day or two, that won't hurt any.

Next we skim off the rose petals. Then we take a clean gallon bottle (called a *secondary fermentor*) and a clean piece of flexible tubing for a siphon (about five feet long). We siphon the liquid from the crock into the bottle to within a few inches of the top. We try to leave most of the sediment behind. Now we take a clean fermentation lock, fill it with water to the line marked on the fermentation lock, and use it to stopper the bottle. We set the bottle aside for a few months. It may continue to work, but very slowly. We aren't hasty.

By the way, we take the dregs left in the crock, dump them into a soda bottle and stopper it with cotton. This will probably produce good wine too, but you never know. (Greer's note: "If this second bottle is full and you see the cotton getting wet, change the cotton. You don't want vinegar bacteria to get started in the cotton stopper itself!")

One more aside: it is possible to concoct a homemade fermentation lock, but since commercial ones are easier to use, readily available, and cheap, I wouldn't bother. Since you may be curious, or desperate, I'll tell you how anyway. One method, going back to Prohibition, is quite simple: take a cork with a hole in it (drill one using a hot screwdriver), put a yard long piece of flexible tubing a few inches through the hole, make an air-tight fit by sealing around the hole with candle-wax or household paraffin, stopper the bottle with the cork (the end of the tube must be *above* the level of the liquid). Run the other end into a soda bottle filled with water. That's it. Another method I've heard of is simplicity itself: tie a balloon over the mouth of the bottle. As the wine works the balloon will expand. As fermentation slows down, it will lose gas and contract. When it is flat, the wine is done. (Greer's note: "Or it has temporarily stopped working because of a temperature change.") For myself, I don't trust the balloon method, and the other is too much trouble with commercial fermentation locks so easy to get and so simple. (The fermentation locks are, of course, reusable.)

Eventually the liquid will be through working. The yeast will die and settle to the bottom of the bottle. The wine will become crystal clear. When it does, it's probably done. But don't be in a hurry, the taste gets better as time goes on.

(Greer's note: "Mel said it is probably done. And he means probably. Sometimes, if the weather turns cold, the yeast will go dormant for a while before it is finished working, then will start up when the weather turns warm again. It really pays not to be in a hurry!") What you should do, though, is siphon the wine away from the sediment in the secondary fermentor into yet another gallon bottle (still called a secondary fermentor), to let it settle again (this is called *racking*). "Top up" in this new bottle with a little water, or any extra wine from that batch that may have gone into a soda bottle earlier. If there's too much air space inside the bottle, the wine may vinegar. Try not to leave more than an inch or so of air below the fermentation lock. (Greer's note: "Better taste that wine in the little bottle to be sure it hasn't vinegared; you never know with just a cotton stopper.") Some people rack several times. We don't; it's a matter of sentiment as well as sediment.

By the way, if you decide the wine is too sweet, try diluting it and letting it ferment again. You may have to add more yeast. Try it without first and see what happens, though.

Before I conclude this discussion let me remark, we would have had plain sugar wine if we had left out the rose petals. It can be flavored with syrups, coffee, for instance, and then it's not bad. Or, instead of rose petals we could have used a few pints of other kinds of edible flower petals: elderblow (elderberry blossoms), cowslips, hawthorn, dandelion, or primrose. Thus we have a whole family of flower wines, all similar to make, though not similar in taste. Let me summarize all this in recipe form:

BASIC FLOWER WINE RECIPE

2 – 3 pints flower petals	2 – 5 pounds sugar
1 gallon water	1 yeast packet

Use rose, elderblow, cowslip, hawthorn, dandelion or prim-
rose. Boil water, stir in sugar. Use chart in Basic Sugar Wine
Recipe to determine amount. Pour into crock and cover.
When cooled to 65° to 70°F, add yeast, then tie plastic over
mouth of crock. Two days later stir in freshly picked flowers.
Let work another twelve days. Then skim out petals, siphon
liquid into gallon bottle and stopper with fermentation lock.
Leave for three months. Then rack into another bottle
(topped up) with fermentation lock. Leave for a year or so.
Then bottle.

   That's it for flower wines. All that's left to discuss is bottling, and that really requires a separate section.

Bottling

   After your wine has been sitting in its secondary fermentor a year or so, it should be crystal clear, and quite done
working. There are some reasons why some wines may not
have cleared by this stage, but certainly all flower wines
should turn clear with no problem. Now it is time to bottle
the wine.

   First you need a supply of bottles that can be securely
corked or capped. Beer bottles and soda bottles do very
nicely. We use the deposit kind, because they are sturdier.
For these you'll need a capper and caps, available from Sears,
Wards, and many other places at not much cost. Don't forget
second-hand stores for a capper. Screw top bottles work well,
provided the tops screw down tightly; that is, the little cardboard insert in the top should be okay. And of course wine
bottles are perfect. And much nicer. You can save them up,
or try bartenders. Or you can buy them by the case from
Sears, Wards, and winemakers supply stores. For wine bottles, you'll need *new* corks and a corker, available at the usual

places: Sears, etc. I'd advise against using half gallon or gallon
bottles. It's too much to have open at one time. But whatever
bottles you pick, make sure you have enough on hand. Figure
it out in advance. For example, suppose you decide to use
12-ounce beer bottles. One gallon is 128 ounces. Twelve into
128 is between 10 and 11, so you'll need ten or eleven bottles
for a gallon. Probably it'll actually be nine or ten, but have
eleven available anyway, just in case.

If possible, a few days ahead of time, put the secondary
fermentor up on a counter or something from which you can
siphon. The sediment you may have stirred up during the
move can resettle. By the way, when you move the secondary fermentor about, try not to turn it. You see, the bottle
turns but the liquid doesn't, so the effect is to stir up any
sediment.

Just before you bottle, it is time to wash the bottles. Dish
washing detergent is all right in *small* quantities, although it
is a little hard to rinse the taste out of the bottles. By far the
best thing to use is a special chlorine detergent made for this
purpose, and available at winemakers' supply stores. It is
quite cheap, and lasts forever (by the way, it doesn't make
suds). Don't use chlorine bleach, it isn't the same thing at all.

Whatever you use, rinse the bottles thoroughly, and let
them drain briefly. Don't worry if they are a little wet inside,
though. Some people are tempted to bake bottles in the oven
to sterilize them or something; don't. It weakens the bottles,
and anyway, it is silly.

There is a handy device that will save lots of time in
washing bottles; it is called a bottle washer. It costs about five
dollars, and is available at winemakers' supply stores. It's
worth it if you have more than a gallon or two to bottle at one
time. It is a simple metal device that is screwed onto a faucet
threaded for a garden hose. It has a tube which points upward. You put a bottle over this tube; the act of doing so
opens a valve and directs a strong spray of water inside the

bottle. Since the bottle is upside-down, the water drains out about as fast as it sprays in. In this way, the bottle is quickly and thoroughly rinsed. Taking the bottle off the device automatically turns the water off.

The routine we've worked out for washing bottles is a simple one. We put what used to be the baby's bathtub inside our bathtub, and fill it with a good splash of chlorine detergent, then water. Our tub faucet is threaded to take a garden hose (I put this faucet on about a year ago—they are available in any hardware store—and it has been a remarkable convenience) and I hook the bottle washer to it. Greer fills the baby's tub with bottles, lets them fill with solution, swishes them about well, empties them back into the tub, and hands the bottles to me. I rinse the bottles using the washer, and set them aside to drain for a moment. We often use beer bottles, so we save cardboard six-pack carriers, and after a few minutes of draining, I put the bottles into the carriers, and they're ready to be used. In this way we can wash fifty bottles in maybe twenty minutes.

To do the actual bottling, you'll need a siphon. There will be sediment in the bottom of the secondary fermentor, so you can't pour from it without stirring that up. A length of plastic or rubber tubing four or five feet long will be fine; I like clear plastic because I can see through it. Wash the siphon in the chlorine detergent. I don't like siphons with rubber bulbs built in; I can never make them work. I just start the siphon going by sucking it full of wine (till there is no air left in the siphon).

Now, starting and stopping the siphon as you bottle may stir up the sediment, so you may first want to siphon the wine away from the sediment into another gallon bottle or crock, then do the actual bottling from that. Or you may not. It is up to you. If you do, wash this other bottle in chlorine detergent, too.

Now, open your secondary fermentor, insert the siphon,

suck it full of wine (it's a good chance to taste it), and stop the
flow by putting your finger over the end or by pinching the
tube. There are available hose clamps which make pinching
the tube quite easy. After you've tried pinching a siphon with
your fingers a few times, you'll appreciate a hose clamp.
Then, carefully push the end of the siphon down into the
secondary fermentor until it clears the sediment to by a
quarter to a half inch. Put the other end into a bottle you wish
to fill, and stop pinching the tube.

You'll notice that the process I have described requires
three hands. Help is often necessary. If the bottle you want
to fill is lower than the secondary fermentor, wine will flow
into it. If it is very much below, wine will flow too fast and
stir up the sediment and flood the room. Two or three feet
is about right. Oh, and if the bottle you are filling is above the
secondary fermentor, the siphon will work backwards. You
have been warned.

When the bottle you wanted to fill has been filled to
within an inch or so of the top, pinch the tube to stop the
flow. Move the siphon end to another bottle and so on.

I find pinching the tube never quite works. I always mess
the floor up, even when I put a bowl under the bottle I'm
filling. So I was overjoyed to find there is a simple device
available to help me fill bottles. It's called a bottle filler. It is
basically a bottle washer, without the means for attaching it
to a faucet. So it winds up being a foot long metal tube, with
some holes in the end. This goes in the end of the siphon.
There is a valve built in, which prevents any wine flow. To
use the thing, insert it in a bottle until the end reaches the
bottom. Push down. This opens the valve, the siphon flows
and the bottle fills. When it is filled, pull the bottle filler out.
This automatically closes the valve, the siphon stops, and
nothing is spilled. It solved a lot of problems for us. Winemakers' supply stores carry bottle fillers. They only cost a few

dollars, and are well worth it. One more thing—you might wonder how to get the siphon going in the first place if the bottle filler with its closed valve is stuck in one end of the tube. What I do is this: I put the end of the bottle filler in my mouth and push the valve button against my teeth. This opens the valve and I then suck the tube full of wine as usual. I know it seems silly, but it works.

One more device you may or may not want to purchase at a winemakers' supply store is a glass tube with a little crook in the end. This goes in the secondary fermentor end of the siphon. With it in place you can simply shove the siphon all the way to the bottom, the crook will insure that you clear the sediment.

By the way, don't throw the sediment away. Put it aside in a soda bottle to settle again. You'll get a glass or so of clear wine from it which you might drink right away (or after a few minutes), or you might add it to any vinegar you are making. This is discussed later.

So now you've got the wine into bottles. The next thing is to seal them. If you've used beer or soda bottles, put new (that's important) bottle caps on with a capper. It is quite fast. Screw top bottles are obvious. If you used wine bottles, you'll need a corker and new corks (this is important, too). You can't simply hammer corks in with a hammer, tempting as it may be. They are made bigger than the openings they are to fill, so a corker squeezes them for insertion. Corkers are cheap, and are available from Sears, Ward's, winemakers' supply stores, and many other places. Follow the instructions that come with yours. Oh, and if the instructions mention a sulphite solution, this means Campden tablets. I talk about them in the section entitled "Refinements."

Once the bottles are sealed, label them. You can paste on homemade labels. You can buy fancy labels with your name printed on them. If you used unmarked bottle caps you can write code numbers on them with magic markers. Or, of course, you could leave off labels altogether and take your chances. Me, I label.

Next, set the bottles aside to age. Wine often gets better as it gets older—within limits, however. One or two years are worth trying for, if you can. Corked wine bottles should be stored on their sides to prevent the corks from drying out. Capped bottles don't need this precaution unless the liner is cork. Most are plastic these days, but look.

One minor bit of advice. Whenever you empty a bottle, rinse it out well. Use a bottle washer if you've got one handy. If not, shake water in it several times. This will make washing bottles a lot easier at bottling time!

And a last bit of advice, this time a major one. Don't be in a hurry about bottling. Wine that's bottled too soon may start fermenting in the bottle (even if it has cleared) especially if the temperature warms up. This produces carbon dioxide gas, which is trapped, and so stays in the bottle. When the bottle is opened, the wine bubbles. This is how champagne is made. A small amount of gas won't hurt. The wine is merely said to be "gassy." In commercial wines it is considered a sign of poor quality. But if too much fermentation goes on in the bottle, the gas could burst the bottle. THIS IS VERY DANGEROUS! Champagne bottles are specially made for strength, and the process of making champagne is carefully controlled. Don't try it yourself unless you are absolutely sure you know what you are doing. And more to the point here, don't bottle your wine before you're sure it's done working. Also, if one bottle bursts, open all the rest of that batch, quickly—also carefully. All this sounds scary, but don't worry. There are stories by the dozens, dating from prohibition, of bursting bottles in the basement. People were in a hurry then. Naturally. But now fermentation locks are easily available, so wine can wait a long time in the secondary fermentor, while it finishes doing its thing. Then it can be bottled with no danger at all. Certainly we've never had any problem. If you have any sense at all, neither will you. I feel I ought to give this warning, but I don't expect it to be necessary.

The Theory and Practice of Dandelion Wine

Dandelion wine is the canonical homemade wine. It can be quite good, and is nothing like any wine you can buy. Everyone knows somebody who has a recipe for dandelion wine, and they're all different. What's more, they all work. What's more, they all give different results. So, dandelion wine is a good example for me to use in describing variations possible in flower winemaking. Think of this section that way.

Earlier I gave a general recipe for flower-flavored sugar wine. If we use dandelion blossoms in that recipe, we get a dandelion wine. This is probably the simplest of all the dandelion wines, though none are very complicated. One comment: instead of two or three pints of blossoms, I like between a half and one gallon of them. A few more comments: the result is supposed to be less bitter if only the petals are used. Few people have the patience for this and I don't think it makes very much difference. But pick them without stems. This is quite easy, just snap off the blossom with your fingernail. It does make for less bitterness. By the way, a friend of ours decided to hire some neighborhood children to pick blossoms for her. They told her they didn't have time. Later they changed their minds and surprised her with gallons of blossoms. All with stems on them. Of course she paid the kids, and then, of course, she felt obliged to use the blossoms. She spent hours pulling off stems. Draw whatever moral you like. To continue with practical advice, pick during the day; in the evening the blossoms are closed and you can't see what bugs you're also getting. One final comment: I think dandelion wine is best as a sweet wine, but only sweet enough to be not dry, not sweet enough to taste sweet. Thus I'd suggest about three pounds of sugar to one gallon of water.

Now for the variations. Remember, the idea is to get the flower flavor into the wine. The method just discussed does this by having the blossoms in the solution during part of the fermentation. Another possibility is this.

ALTERNATE FLOWER WINE INSTRUCTIONS

Pour boiling water over the blossoms (no sugar) and leave them to soak for three to five days. Stir well every day, or it may begin to smell pretty bad (that happened to a batch we started). If any mold forms on top, skim it off. After three to five days, strain out the blossoms. Now we have flower flavored water, and we proceed just as if we were making sugar wine. We add our sugar, yeast, and let it work as in the Basic Sugar Wine Recipe.

I've discussed two ways of getting the flower flavor into the wine, one uses blossoms before fermentation, the other during. The only other possibility is after fermentation. This is how coffee wine can be made. I suppose you could steep flower petals in finished sugar wine for a few days to get the flavor into the liquid. We've never tried it ourselves. (Greer's note: "Or you can bruise some petals, or mint, or some other herb and put them in the bottom of your wine glass and fill it up with sugar wine, for a very delicate flavor. My own taste would be to chill the concoction for a few minutes before serving it.")

We've said all there is to say about getting dandelion

flavor into the wine. The next topic is how to modify that flavor. One common problem with homemade wine is that it isn't acid enough. One common remedy in making dandelion wine is to throw in some citrus fruit while it works. For instance, suppose we follow any of the dandelion wine recipes given above, but just before the yeast is added we throw in two or three cut up oranges and two or three cut up lemons, or the juice from them, or even bottled lemon juice. Then let it work. This alters things quite a bit. Grapefruit can also be used, but we've found it tends to flavor the final product strongly, so go easy. (Greer says, "Better yet, leave it out!") Also, you may find adding rinds makes for bitterness. Then again, you may not. By the way, with all this stuff in the brew, your primary fermentor should be a gallon or two bigger than the amount of wine you're after.

Another possible variant is adding raisins. This tends to add "body" to the wine. It "thickens it up." I like the result. Tastes vary, though. The way it is done is simple: follow any of the dandelion wine recipes given above, then after the sugar has gone in but before the yeast, add one half to one pound of raisins, preferably chopped. Wheat can also be used (in the same amount and in the same way), but I've never tried it. (Greer says I should say this is wheat as it comes from the farmer, not sprouted or cracked or ground into flour. I don't think it needs saying, so I won't.)

Finally, considerable variation is possible in how long the various additions are to be left in. Depending on your taste, the citrus fruit can be scooped out (and squeezed) after a week. The raisins can be added part way through the fermentation. All things are possible. As an example of a recipe with all sorts of variations present, I'll give the recipe for dandelion wine I tried as a teen-ager. It's still the one I like best.

DANDELION WINE OF MY YOUTH

3 quarts blossoms	4 pounds sugar
2 oranges, sliced	1 gallon boiling water
2 lemons, sliced	1 yeast cake
1 pound raisins	

Pour water over blossoms, citrus fruit, and sugar. When cooled add dissolved yeast cake. Let stand for seven days stirring well once a day. Strain. Add raisins. Let stand until it stops working. Strain again and bottle.

Some comments. Notice this calls for three quarts of blossoms. A gallon is possible if more flower flavor is desired. Also two oranges and two lemons are called for. More could be used. This calls for four pounds of sugar. The result is a slightly sweet wine. I find it quite pleasant, but three pounds of sugar would give a drier though still good recipe. This recipe, which is an old one, calls for one yeast cake. I always use dried yeast. Also, this recipe calls for raisins. The resulting wine is a deep, rich amber in color. Without the raisins, it is a paler gold. Finally, this recipe calls for bottling when done working. Today, after two or three weeks I'd strain out the raisins (Greer says: "Put them in raisin bread or rice pudding for a memorable result!!"), put the stuff in a gallon bottle with a fermentation lock, and leave it for a long, long time before bottling.

Okay, now you know the variations possible with dandelion wine. All of them are also possible with all the other flower wines I mentioned. There are few hard and fast rules. Indeed, the only one I can think of is that raisins tend to hide the flavor of some flowers. Go easy. Otherwise the only guide is your taste. Anything will work, it's just that you'll like some things more than others.

Grocery Store Winemaking

So far I've only talked about wines made from flowers. It's possible to make wine from virtually any edible fruit or berry, and it is quite easy too. The main new complication added is simply this: fruit has some sugar of its own which must be taken into account. I assume you'll want to make wine from the fruits of your fields. Everybody has this alcoholic Garden of Eden wish where winemaking is concerned. But, to simplify the discussion (and for those of you who don't yet have fields), I'll begin by talking about winemaking using canned juices from the grocery store.

Recently I bought some cans of a standard brand apricot nectar from the market. This has sugar added, which probably means that seasonal variations in sweetness do not occur, they are evened out by the canner. The cans I bought acted as if they contained one and a half pounds of sugar to the gallon. (I'll say how I knew this in a later section.) Probably any can of that brand apricot nectar I buy at any time will act like it has one and a half pounds of sugar to the gallon in it. Now, what about winemaking? I decided to try for a dry apricot wine. I dumped one gallon of apricot nectar into a crock straight from the can. Now I had a solution with the equivalent of one and a half pounds of sugar present. I wanted about two and a half pounds of sugar for a dry wine (using figures from the Basic Sugar Wine Recipe) so I added a another pound of sugar. Then I proceeded just as if it were sugar wine. I dumped in yeast, let it work for five or six days, then siphoned it into a bottle with a fermentation lock, and so on. You might ask, why begin with a crock, since there are no blossoms to worry about? The reason is: the first few days of fermentation are very vigorous. In a bottle, foam might clog the fermentation lock. Later on, things will settle down and a bottle can be used.

Similar techniques work with any store-bought juice with sugar added. For your convenience here's a chart of figures I've found works well. The right-hand column gives the average amount of sugar I've found already present.

DRINK	POUNDS SUGAR PER GALLON PRESENT
apricot nectar	1 1/2
cranberry juice coctail	1 1/2
cranapple	2

Just use this chart together with the earlier information and you should be okay. For instance, suppose you want a medium sweet cranberry wine. Well, medium sweet calls for, say three and a half pounds of sugar per gallon. So just add another two pounds of sugar to a gallon and go at it. Please remember, though: these figures are all convenient approximations. I'll tell you later on how to be more accurate, but it is more work. If you want to do things this simple way, keep records so you can work out figures that suit your own tastes. Use mine as convenient starting points. Once you get *your* recipes worked out, everything is trivial. And working them out is fun.

Now, one more complication: some store-bought juices have no sugar added. Apple juice is a good example. This means the sweetness may vary from brand to brand and from year to year. I've worked out a chart for some juices in this category, but be aware of these possible variations. Also be aware that if you make a dry wine when you want a sweet one, it's fair to add more sugar when you drink it, and if you made a sweet wine when you want a dry one, somebody will like it. So here's my chart for juices with no sugar added, with the understanding that figures different from these may occur.

JUICE	POUNDS SUGAR PER GALLON PRESENT
apple	1 1/4 – 1 1/2
purple grape	1 3/4 (can vary considerably)
prune	2 – 2 1/4

Some remarks: supermarket grape juice makes a decent dry wine; dry apple wine is not very good. If the fruit taste of wine made from canned juices is too strong for you, dilute the juice before fermenting. Figuring the amount of sugar in the diluted juice is easy. For example, suppose you are using a juice having two pounds of sugar per gallon of liquid. Suppose also that you decide to use three quarts of juice and one quart of water. Well, you don't have one gallon of pure juice, you have used three-quarters of a gallon (three quarts out of four), so you don't have two pounds of sugar present, you have three-quarters of two pounds, or one and a half pounds.

Now let me summarize the procedures of this section in recipe form.

BASIC STORE BOUGHT JUICE RECIPE

1 gallon commercially canned fruit juice
sugar
1 yeast packet

Dump juice in crock. Use charts in this section to determine how much sugar is probably present. Use chart in Basic Sugar Wine Recipe to determine how much extra sugar to add. Add sugar; when dissolved, add yeast. Cover crock with plastic. After five to six days, siphon liquid into gallon bottle with fermentation lock. Rack after three months, bottle in about one year.

Well, so much for supermarket sipping. This should keep you happy until you get around to putting your orchard and vineyard into shape.

A Ramble Through the Brambles

We are finally face to face with basic reality, making wine from real fruit, not fruit that some company has picked and washed and squeezed and canned for you. This adds another complication to those of earlier sections, namely, the juice isn't in a can, it's still in the fruit. Somehow the taste has to be gotten out. I'll say how shortly, but before that, one further difficulty: wine can be made with a stronger or a weaker fruit taste. What is wanted will vary from person to person. Canned fruit juice is aimed at, and generally hits, the average taste. But with fresh fruit, you have all the options yourself. The upshot is that I can't be as precise as I was in earlier sections. I can't say strawberries have just so much sugar, since you may want a stronger strawberry taste than I want, and so may use more strawberries. Also, strawberries will vary in sugar content considerably from season to season, variety to variety, and place to place, and with size. All sorts of variables. No, the best I can do now is to give a general recipe for you to use as a starting point. Keep records and you'll soon modify it to suit your own taste. But in the next chapter, I'll say how to get some precise control back, even with fresh fruit.

One possibility for winemaking from fresh fruit is to squeeze the juice out, then ferment that, maybe with sugar and water added. It works, and is ideal for grape wine. The general recipe I propose is less work, however, and I'd suggest it for everything except grapes. Since the specific fruit doesn't matter, I'll simply say "fruit."

BASIC FRUIT WINE RECIPE

2 – 3 pounds fruit	2 – 3 pounds sugar
1 gallon water	1 packet yeast

Take the fruit, pit and stem it if that's appropriate. Peel it if pectin is a problem (see below). Crush the fruit up in a crock (or cut it up, if appropriate). Dump one gallon of hot water on it. Mush it around, then stir in the sugar. Let it cool off, then stir in the yeast. Cover it but stir it once a day. After five or six days scoop out the fruit (squeezing is still fair) siphon wine into a gallon bottle and continue as with Basic Store Bought Juice Wine Recipe (note the similarity in procedure between this and my teen-age dandelion wine).

A few comments. First, pectin is a problem. See the chapter where jelly making is discussed for information about it. In jelly making, pectin is wanted; here it isn't, since it makes for cloudy wine. The simplest precaution is to make sure you only use *fully ripe fruit.* Underripe fruit contains more pectin, you see. Also, peel apples and pears and core them because there's lots of pectin there. (Greer's note: use the peels and cores for jell.) Second, some fruits contribute less taste this way than others, so I suggest you use twice the amount of fruit called for if you are making strawberry wine, and three times the amount if apple.

Simple, isn't it? Now, what variations are possible? Well, this recipe generally produces a dry wine with a light fruit taste. If you want a stronger fruit taste, use more fruit. Double or triple the amounts involved. Also, you may want a sweeter wine. A sweet wine with a strong fruit taste is rather like a cordial. If this is your desire, use more sugar, of course. Also, adding raisins is allowed. Suit your tastes. But don't forget, fruit varies in sugar content from year to year and from location to location, so even if you always follow the same recipe, your wine may not always taste the same. Still, the variation won't be great, so when you work out a recipe you like, stick with it. And if that's not good enough, there is a method for determining the amount of sugar naturally present in the fruit you are using. That's the subject for another chapter, though.

CHAPTER 12

WINES
TO MAKE
WHEN
YOU'RE SOBER

Mel speaking

Getting Technical—The Hydrometer

By now you know that the strength and sweetness of the wine you make depend on the amount of sugar in the fruit juice you start with. So it's important to know how much sugar you've got, and if nobody tells you, how are you going to find out? It turns out that there's a simple technique for doing just this. You may have already learned it in high school chemistry, but don't let that intimidate you. The whole procedure is about as complicated as using a meat thermometer in cooking a roast.

199

You know, of course, that if you dissolve sugar or salt, say, in water, the solution is "thicker" than water. Denser is the proper term. Now, something that floats will float higher in this denser solution than it will in plain water. You float better in sea water than in fresh water, for example. Measuring how high something floats in a sugar solution as compared to how high it floats in plain water can tell you how much sugar is in the solution. A hydrometer is a device which does this sort of measurement quite simply.

A hydrometer is a long glass tube, weighted on one end so that it floats upright. You float it in the solution you're interested in, and how high it floats tells you how dense the solution is, and hence how much sugar is in it. It has a scale of numbers printed on it; all you have to do is read the one at the surface of the solution. That's pretty simple. I should mention that hydrometers are available from Sears Roebuck, Montgomery Ward, and winemakers' supply stores. They cost about five dollars.

I should also mention that there are other things in fruit juice besides sugar, and a hydrometer lumps all these things together with the sugar, without differentiating; so it isn't strictly accurate for determining sugar content. But these other things are minor in comparison to the amount of sugar present, so they can be safely ignored. I will talk as if only the sugar has an effect.

Next, I should mention the units in which hydrometers are marked. You are interested in the amount of sugar present. I've been giving such amounts in pounds per gallon, but a hydrometer isn't marked that way. Hydrometers can be used to measure the density of all kinds of liquids, not just sugar solutions, so they are marked in a way that is independent of sugar. What they tell you directly is how much heavier a given volume of what you're measuring is than the same volume of water. This is called *specific gravity*. For example, to say the specific gravity of a certain liquid is 1.3 is simply to say that a gallon of it is 1.3 times heavier than a gallon of water. Then water winds up with a specific gravity of exactly 1. Hydrometers tell you the specific gravity of the liquid you are measuring. There are tables that can be used to convert this to a sugar reading, but it isn't really necessary to do so. Many wine recipes don't say "begin with so much sugar in so much water," rather they say, "begin with a solution whose specific gravity is such and so." Information is given directly in terms of specific gravity. For example, instead of saying two to two and three-quarter pounds of sugar in a gallon of water will make a dry sugar wine, I could say a sugar solution whose specific gravity is between 1.075 and 1.100 will make a dry wine. This is a more useful kind of information since it works even if we are fermenting a fruit juice made from fresh fruit, and not a plain sugar solution we mixed up. So, from now on, all my discussions will be in terms of specific gravity, not in pounds of sugar per gallon.

A slight complication. For certain purposes other scales besides specific gravity are sometimes used. These days many winemaking hydrometers have several scales printed on them. Specific gravity is all that need concern us there.

There are two additional pieces of equipment which help in using a hydrometer. The first is a gravy baster. This is a good thing for getting liquid out from under a floating mass of fruit pulp, and from bottles, for testing. The second is a testing jar. This is simply a tall, clear-sided plastic jar in which the rather long hydrometer can float upright without needing a great amount of liquid. They are available where hydrometers are sold. Indeed, they often come with the hydrometer.

Before I get into the main use of hydrometers—sugar adjustment—I should mention that they are also useful for deciding when fermentation of *dry* wines is over. When the specific gravity of a fermenting liquid has dropped to a little below 1.000, the dry wine is done. You see, all the sugar is gone now. Its place has been taken by alcohol which is slightly less dense than water.

Now let me describe in detail the main use of a hydrometer. Let's say I have a gallon of grape juice to ferment, either store bought or squeezed from my own grapes. I know nothing about the sugar content of this juice, so what should I do? Well, I fill the testing jar to within a few inches of the top with grape juice and lower in the hydrometer. Air bubbles clinging to it may throw off the reading, so I give it a good spin to shake them off. When it comes to rest I observe what number on the scale is at the surface of the grape juice. (There is a quirk, however. Because of surface tension the juice will climb slightly up the stem of the hydrometer. Ignore this. Mentally extend the flat surface of the juice and see where it would cross the hydrometer if no such "climbing" occurred. That's the proper reading. In practice, the difference is slight, fortunately.)

So, I get a reading. Let's say it was 1.052 (most available hydrometers read to three decimal places). But this is not necessarily the specific gravity of the juice. How high things float also depends on temperature. Hydrometers have a temperature at which they are right (often 60°F). For other temperatures, corrections must be made. So the next step is to take out the hydrometer and stick in a thermometer. Let's say the temperature turns out to be 70°F. According to a simple correction table that comes with the hydrometer I should add .001. So the specific gravity of the grape juice is actually 1.052 + .001 or 1.053. This temperature correction never amounts to much for temperatures within 10° of the "right" temperature for the hydrometer, so for rough measures, if the juice is at room temperature, and that is near the "right" hydrometer temperature, I skip the temperature correction. If I'm measuring liquids which have recently been heated, temperature correction is necessary.

A comment: it is common for winemakers to drop the "1." from the specific gravity readings. Then 1.053 would simply appear as 53. This is a convenient shorthand. It is general to use the term "degree" if this convention is used. Thus, the grape juice has a specific gravity of 53 degrees. Don't confuse this with temperature degrees, I am talking about specific gravity.

So, I've got a grape juice whose specific gravity is 53 degrees. What next? Well, the following chart tells what kinds of wine will be produced, in terms of the specific gravities of the starting solutions.

TYPE OF WINE	SPECIFIC GRAVITY OF STARTING SOLUTION IN DEGREES	EQUIVALENT AMOUNT OF SUGAR PER GALLON
dry	75 – 95	2 1/2
dry, but strong	95 – 100	2 1/2 – 2 3/4
dividing line	110	3
slightly sweet	115 – 120	3 1/4 – 3 1/2
medium sweet	120 – 140	3 1/2 – 4
very sweet	140 – 170	4 – 5

Note: Extremes are bad. A dry wine shouldn't be as strong as possible; 90–95 degrees is about right. Also a sweet wine shouldn't be as sweet as possible. Don't forget, you can always add extra sugar later on, if it isn't sweet enough for you.

Please note, too, that these figures work for me. Keep records and you'll soon find what works best for you. For one thing, what you consider slightly sweet, I might call medium sweet. The terms mean different things to different people.

For another thing, no measuring device is perfect. Your hydrometer might have a systematic error of a few degrees one way, and mine of a few degrees another. As I say, keep records, and decide what's best for you.

Now, let's say I want a dry wine. I decide to aim at a specific gravity of between 90 and 95 degrees, let's say 93 for convenience, since the grape juice I just measured had a specific gravity of 53 degrees. This means I have to add enough sugar to raise the specific gravity of my gallon of grape juice by 93 minus 53, or 40 degrees. How much sugar should I add? Well, a good rule of thumb, accurate enough if the amounts involved are not great, is the following.

Rule 1. Four ounces of sugar added to 1 gallon raises specific gravity 10 degrees.

According to this rule, since I want a rise of 4 × 10 or 40 degrees, I should add 4 × 4 or 16 ounces of sugar, that is, 1 pound. (If I wanted a rise of 40 degrees, but I only had half a gallon, I would use half the amount of sugar called for, or 1/2 pound. Likewise, if I wanted a rise of only 5 degrees, or 1/2 × 10, I ought to add 1/2 × 4 or 2 ounces of sugar. This rule is accurate for small amounts, say up to about 1 1/2 pounds of sugar.)

So, I stir 1 pound of sugar into my gallon of grape juice, dissolving it well. Now the specific gravity should be 93, which is just what I wanted. If I'm nervous, I could check it again with the hydrometer, and make any minor adjustments by adding more sugar, or by diluting with water as appropriate. But remember, anything between 90 and 95 is fine; it isn't that critical. Let's say I hit 93 exactly, to make things simple.

To summarize so far: I have a gallon of grape juice to which I have added 1 pound of sugar, raising its specific gravity to 93, which will produce a dry wine. Now, I still have a gallon of liquid, right? Wrong. I added sugar. This increased the volume. This is good to know when deciding what to put the stuff in for the secondary fermentation. Well, how much have I got? For this there's another rule of thumb.

Rule 2. One pound of sugar added to a solution increases the volume by 1 1/4 cups.

So I have 1 1/4 cups over a gallon. It won't fit in a gallon bottle for the secondary fermentation. I'll use a gallon bottle for most of it, with a fermentation lock, and put the rest in a soda bottle, stoppered with cotton.

From here on, things are standard. I dump the sweetened grape juice into a crock, add yeast, cover, let it work for a week, then siphon it into a secondary fermentor and so on.

Well, there it is. By using the hydrometer and Rule 1, I was able to calculate easily the right amount of sugar to add to get the wine I wanted. And the whole process only took a few minutes. In fact, it was by just this sort of procedure that I worked out the sugar contents of the fruit juices that I gave in the section on grocery store winemaking.

This is the first section in which I've discussed making grape wine from real grapes. The reason, of course, is that sugar content varies so greatly from region to region and with grape variety that either a hydrometer or lots and lots of experience is necessary. Well, now the hydrometer has been discussed, and I can give in detail recipes for grape wine.

BASIC RED WINE RECIPE

grapes
sugar
yeast

Remove stems from grapes. Put in a big crock and crush well. A good tool to use is a masher consisting of a small piece of plank nailed to the end of a 2 × 4. Remove some juice and test specific gravity, but add no sugar yet. Stir in yeast, cover and let ferment. Twice a day stir and push down the floating caps of skins and pulp. After three to six days (that is, when the juice is as red as you want) siphon off the juice. Also, press the juice out of the pulp with a wine press. Measure the volume of juice, and add sugar according to the earlier specific gravity reading, using the chart and Rule 1. Put juice in secondary fermentors, but leave about one-eighth empty. Stopper with cotton. After vigorous fermentation stops (maybe three weeks) siphon the juice off the sediment, again into big bottles. This time fill them to within an inch of the top. Fit them with fermentation locks. Rack in about two months (topping up). If possible leave in cellar just above freezing (this helps the wine to clear). Rack again toward spring. Bottle in autumn.

Greer's note: "Using a wine press is easy. What I do is this. I put the fruit to be pressed into a pillowcase, and the pillowcase into the body of the wine press. The press itself I put on a large kettle which I've set up in the bathtub in case of spills. I fit the lid down inside the press, start screwing down the large screw bar until it fits into its hole in the lid. Then I give it a few more turns. I know I've turned it enough when the juice starts dripping out. Once the juice has started flowing, I go off and do something else for ten minutes or so, checking every so often to see if the juice has stopped running. When it has, I turn the screw down some more, again until the juice is running, and again go off and do other things. I repeat this until I can't screw it down any more (it gets very tight after a while). I call on Mel to give it its last couple of turns. When we've got all the juice we think we'll get, I unscrew it, lift out the lid, take the pillowcase out and hose down the wine press with very hot water. That's all there is to it. Back to Melvin."

Some comments: Keep the wine at about 70° during

fermentation. The amount of juice varies with the variety of grape. Roughly thirteen to sixteen pounds of grapes give a gallon. Sugar content of grape juice also varies considerably. Northeast grapes will need sugar, California grapes may need water to bring the sugar level down. This recipe won't, of course, produce red wine from white grapes.

BASIC WHITE WINE RECIPE

Grapes
Sugar
Yeast

Remove stems from grapes. Put in a big crock and crush well (see above recipe). Press grapes using wine press, and collect the juice (discarding skin and pulp). Allow juice to settle overnight, and siphon away from sediment. Measure specific gravity and adjust sugar content. Add yeast and put juice into bottles, leaving them one-eighth to one-quarter empty. Stopper with cotton. When vigorous fermentation ends, siphon juice away from sediment, into nearly full bottles. Stopper with fermentation locks. Rack in about two months. Rack again toward spring (top up each time). If possible, leave in cellar just above freezing. Bottle about autumn.

Some comments: Keep at around 70°F during fermentation. This recipe won't give a white wine if the juice is red. Notice, the main difference between this recipe and the red wine recipe is that here no fermentation occurs with skins or pulp present.

Greer's note: "For reasons of economy you might want to do the following. Measure the amount of juice you pressed out of the grapes for the white wine. Then measure out half that amount of water and put it into the pulp and skins, mush it around, and either ferment this according to the red wine recipe, or strain it and can it up as grape drink or make jell.

If you make it into wine, it will be of poorer quality than the "first run," but it will be drinkable. And if you don't like it, you can make it into wine vinegar, which is getting expensive these days. It's worth a try, anyway."

Now let's resume discussion of the hydrometer. I said Rule 1 was not accurate for large amounts. Why not? And what's better? Well, let me first give you a more accurate rule, which I find even easier to use than Rule 1. This new rule is in graph form, which is why it is easy to use: no calculation is involved. I worked the graph out mostly because it's the way I'm built. Doing this sort of thing is fun for me. I spent two evenings dumping sugar into water and on the floor, and taking specific gravity readings, then another three days recalling my college Differential Equations course from years ago. But the result of all that is a graph that saves a little calculation from time to time. Mathematicians are lazy people, you see.

In the graph on page 209, along the bottom are pounds of sugar, and along the side the degrees of specific gravity by which one gallon of liquid will be raised by the addition of the corresponding amount of sugar.

Suppose, as in the grape juice example, that I want to raise the specific gravity by 40 degrees. I find 40 on the left-hand scale. The 40-degree line hits the curve above the 1-pound sugar mark, so I add 1 pound. I get the amount of sugar to add without any calculations at all. But notice, to raise specific gravity by 80 degrees doesn't require 2 pounds of sugar, as Rule 1 would have. Rather, the graph says we need between 2 and 2 1/4 pounds (which is not greatly different, however).

The main practical value of this graph is that it does the calculations for me. The difference between what it recommends and what Rule 1 calls for is not much ordinarily. So consider it a time saver. Its greater accuracy isn't very impor-

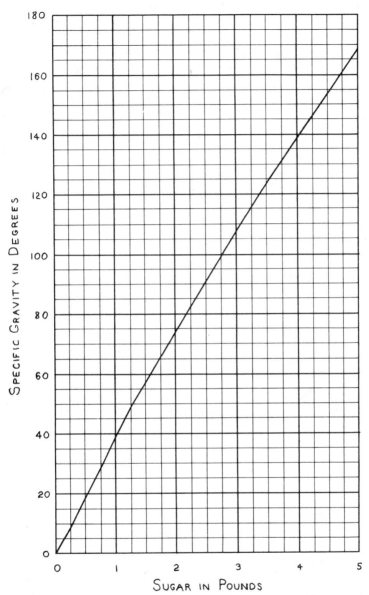

This chart is for estimating the amount of sugar to add in
winemaking. For details refer to the surrounding text.

tant in practice. But why is it different from Rule 1? The reason is simple. Suppose I have 1 gallon of water. Its specific gravity is 1.000, or 0 degrees. Suppose I add 1 pound of sugar. By Rule 1, I now have a solution whose specific gravity is 40. But, I no longer have a gallon of liquid, rather, by Rule 2, I have 1 1/4 cups more than a gallon, so Rule 1 doesn't apply. If I throw away 1 1/4 cups, then add the second pound of sugar, I would have a specific gravity of 80. Otherwise the specific gravity must be something less than 80 since the second pound of sugar was added to a larger quantity of liquid than one gallon. The net result is that while 1 pound of sugar can raise specific gravity by 40 degrees, 2 pounds won't quite raise it by 80. Rule 1 is accurate enough for small amounts, but for large amounts, Rule 2 throws it off.

The following is extra, and has nothing to do with wine-making. It's just an illustration of the way mathematics enters into everything, including drinking. I am a mathematician. When faced with the sort of situation I've just described it is natural for me to try and come up with a replacement for Rule 1 which works for large quantities as well as small. I did so; nothing is needed beyond very elementary differential equations. If you had such a course in college and want to review it, try the following.

Assume Rule 1 and Rule 2 are correct for small quantities, and derive that the formula of the graph is

$$y = 512 \ln \left(1 + \frac{10x}{128}\right).$$

Happy drinking.

Getting Technicaler—Acid Control

Now you know all about the hydrometer, so you can make wines to suite your tastes. And that's the end of it? Not quite. There are many things besides sugar that affect wine taste, and one of the most important of these is acid. A wine that's not acid enough will taste rather dull; a wine that's too acid will taste, well, too acid. And, as it happens, the acid content of homemade wine can be controlled with only a little extra work.

I suppose you should know that there are many kinds of acids that can be present in fruit juice: citric, malic, tartaric, tannic, and others. Fortunately there is no need to consider them separately. It is customary to pick one kind as a standard and talk as if all the other acids had been converted to equivalent amounts (strengths) of that one. This means I can talk about general acid content without specifying which acids I'm talking about. In the United States, tartaric acid is the standard.

All you need to know in practice is: how can you tell how much acid is in fruit juice; how much ought there be, how does the acid content get changed?

How can you tell how much acid is present? There is only one practical way for home use: buy an acid testing kit. Sears, Ward's, and winemaking supply stores carry them. They cost five or six dollars. Using one of these kits is probably the most complicated procedure connected with winemaking. But it is not very difficult after all, and makes for better wine. As a bonus, the kits can also be used to measure the strength of homemade vinegar; that's discussed in another section. All the kits come with complete instructions (which differ slightly from brand to brand) so I won't say any more about them.

Next, how much acid ought there be? Here are general guidelines. For fruit or flower wines the juice to be fermented should have an acid content of about .6% (that's 6 *tenths* of a percent, not six percent). For red grape wines the content should be higher, .65%, and for white .7%. These figures can, of course, be changed to suit your own taste.

Finally, what should be done if the acid content of whatever is to be fermented is not correct? If it is too low, simply add some appropriate acid. There is avilable from Sears, Ward's, and winemakers' supply stores a powder called *acid blend*. This is a mixture of citric, malic and tartaric acid. The amount to add will be small, a teaspoonful or so. Work it out by trial and error for best results. Acid blend is ideal for grape wines, but for fruit and flower wines you could just add citric acid, which is available in many places, drug stores and some grocery stores included. In general you'll need more citric acid than acid blend to get the same result. Or, finally, you could throw citrus fruits into the juice to be fermented. I mentioned this back in the dandelion wine section. Cut up some oranges and lemons and stir them in well. Or, if you like, squeeze the juice out of them, or use bottled lemon juice, then measure the effect of this on the acid content of the liquid you are fermenting. I can't give any formulas for this since the acid (it's citric, of course) varies from lemon to lemon.

If the acid content is too high, try diluting with water. There is an easy way to determine how much water to add. Take the percentage by which you want to reduce the acid content, and divide it by the percentage of acid you want to wind up with. This gives you the fraction you must add. For example, suppose I've got one gallon of currant juice, the acid content of which is .9% and I want it to be .6%. Well, the amount by which the acid content should be reduced is .9 minus .6 or .3. That, divided by the percentage of acid I want is .3/.6 or 1/2. Therefore I should add a half gallon of water, that is, half the volume of the juice.

Instead of water, some people add calcium carbonate to neutralize some of the acid (available from winemaking supply stores). It forms a salt which settles out and so is not present in the finished product. It can be used together with added water, if that is desired. First add some calcium carbonate; this reduces the acid level by a certain amount. Measure the acid level again, then you can figure out how much water will bring it down the rest of the way. But you shouldn't add more than two teaspoons of calcium carbonate per gallon or the taste may be affected. Sometimes even less can affect the taste. I suspect that as the salt formed settles out, it drags down with it other things which make for good taste; I'm not sure about this. I don't use calcium carbonate myself.

Adding much water can make for a "thin" wine; adding calcium carbonate can affect taste. Then what do you do with a very high-acid juice? Simple. Take a low-acid juice (not necessarily the same kind; be daring) and mix them. The mixture won't take much acid adjusting.

Having mixed a high- and low-acid juice together, you could measure the acid content of the mixture, of course, but it is a nuisance, and it really isn't necessary. There's a simple way of calculating the acid content of the mixture without any more measuring. Here it is. Take the percent of acid in the first juice and multiply it by the amount of that juice you have. (The result is a measure of how much acid you're getting from that juice.) Do the same with the second kind of juice. Add the two numbers together (this is a measure of how much acid you are getting from both juices). Divide that number by the amount of juice in the mixture and the result is the percent of acid in it.

Let me give you an example. This fall Greer promised to gather some sumac berries. We'd made sumac wine last year. It had possibilities, but it was terribly acid. We thought a sumac-apple wine might be more to our tastes. What with one thing and another, we got apples but no sumac berries. But we did pick eight bushels of tomatoes from our garden. They weren't ripe, but the radio predicted hail for that day,

so Greer got them in. We spread out the tomatoes upstairs
to ripen. Greer thought she'd can them in a leisurely fashion
as they ripened up, and all would be well. But one thing and
another came up—and the tomatoes reached—and passed—
their peak. Greer tried everything fast she could think of to
use them up. There was no time to can them. The impact
that this sorry tale had on the present section is a certain
tomato-apple wine experiment. Here we were blending two
juices out of desperation, not for acid adjustment, but the
calculations were the same.

I had eleven cups of apple juice at .3% acid, and six cups
of tomato juice at .6% acid. I dumped the juices together.
What was the acid content of the mixture? Well, for the apple
juice I multiplied 11 by .3 getting 3.3. For the tomato juice
I multiplied 6 by .6 getting 3.6. I added these together, getting 6.9. The mixture amounted to seventeen cups, so I divided 6.9 by 17, getting about .4. So the mixture had an acid
content of .4%. I think the wine may be a good one, odd as
it sounds.

The only thing to remember in these calculations is:
measure everything the same way. Don't measure one juice
in cups and the other in quarts. Measure both in quarts or
both in cups, or both in liters, or whatever. Then you should
be all right.

Refinements

What I've told you so far will get you good wine almost
all the time. In this section I'll discuss some simple refinements in technique which may make for even better wine.

The only yeast I've so far suggested you use is baker's
yeast. There are lots of different yeasts, and baker's yeast,
while good for baking, is not the best for winemaking. You

can get yeasts that are ideal for wines from Sears, Ward's, and winemakers' supply stores. They generally come dried, in packets, just like baker's yeast. The best for most use is called "All Purpose Wine Yeast." Use it just as you did the baker's yeast. The results will be better and the cost about the same.

If you wish to get really fanatic about winemaking, it is possible to get special purpose wine yeasts, each aimed at a particular kind of wine: Bordeaux, Burgundy, Sherry, Bernkastler, and so on. Presumably these are the strains of yeasts used to make the respective wines. These are more delicate than the all purpose wine yeast, and require a "starter" rather like a bread starter in baking. Also some experience is necessary to know when to use what. So I won't say any more about them here. An all-purpose wine yeast is your best bet.

The most fermented fruit in the world is the grape. This is not accidental. Wine yeast works best on grape juice. Grape juice usually contains enough sugar and enough acid to make good wine. Well, we've already discussed adjusting the sugar and acid of fruit juice. But also, grape juice contains other things that keep yeast happy, things analogous to vitamins and minerals to us. Most other fruit juices don't have enough of these things, so it is best to add them. The idea is to approximate grape juice in everything except taste. Doing this is simple. From the usual places, just buy a supply of yeast nutrient tablets or powder. These are mostly ammonium salts. Two or three tablets in a gallon of liquid should be enough, though fresh grape juice won't need any. To use the tablets, put them on a piece of paper and crush them to a fine powder with the bowl of a spoon. Then dump them into the juice you are going to ferment. Yeast will work without yeast nutrient, but it will work a lot better with it.

For centuries it has been the practice to sterilize wine barrels by burning sulphur inside them. These days the key part of the process is available in tablet form, under the name of Campden tablets. These consist of a sulphur containing compound, sodium bisulfite or potassium metabisulphite, for instance. When dissolved they release a tiny quantity of sulphur dioxide, the same gas that results when sulphur is burned. This kills wild yeast, but not wine yeast (I don't know about baker's yeast) so it makes winemaking a surer thing. All commercial wineries use a "sulphiting" chemical in their freshly squeezed grape juice, and if you're a label reader, you'll find it is in some store-bought juices. Campden tablets are used just as nutrient tablets are, that is, crush them with a spoon, and stir them into the juice before you ferment it. One or two tablets per gallon should be fine. Probably none will be necessary with store-bought fruit juice, since it was sterilized when it was canned. Also, if the idea of adding things to the wine bothers you, don't. You may make poorer wine once in a while, but you'll still get good stuff most of the time.

Some fruit contains lots of pectin, apples for instance. Certain cookbooks (*Joy of Cooking* is one) have charts showing the amounts of pectin in various fruits. Wines made from these fruits may remain cloudy. This doesn't affect the taste, but it is not nice aesthetically. There is an enzyme available from winemakers' supply stores that breaks down pectin. This is added to the juice before it is fermented. Follow the instructions on the label. You might also try adding it to a cloudy fruit wine that will not clear, if you suspect pectin is the problem.

There are other things that can be added if you wish. Sears Roebuck, for instance, carries Clarifier tablets and Preservative tablets. Clarifier tablets probably help the sediment settle out. Wine books discuss such things under the name of "finings." Unflavored gelatin can be used for this, and in the old days egg whites were used. Preservative tablets keep wine from turning dark in the bottle. Probably they are ascorbic acid, which is also used in home freezing. I say probably because I've never bought them. Campden tablets are also used for this purpose. One tablet per gallon at bottling time should serve. Sometimes both ascorbic acid and Campden tablets are used. I can't comment on any of this since I've never had trouble getting wine clear, and I've never added anything at bottling time. If any of my wine ever turns unpleasantly dark, I'll probably start, though. We do make sure to use fully ripe fruit for winemaking, however.

A few other bits and pieces of things will finish out the section. First, most store-bought grape juice is not made from grapes that are the best for winemaking. If you want good traditional—meaning grape—wine, and don't have your own vines, you may want to get grape concentrate especially prepared for winemakers. (A side note: the best wine grapes don't grow in the Northeast.) Sears and Ward's and winemakers' supply stores carry these concentrates. Also elderberry, gooseberry, and other concentrates are available at winemakers' supply stores, as are dried blossoms of various sorts for flower wines.

Finally, don't be afraid to mix your wines after they're done. I've already mentioned mixing juices before fermentation to get the acid right. After wines are made, you can blend wines to suit your taste. A wine too sweet and one too dry might go well together. (But don't bottle the mixture right away. Put it under a fermentation lock: it might start working again.) Or you might mix wines just to see how the tastes blend. It may take some time: a few weeks to a few months for mixed wines to "marry," so don't be in a hurry to judge the results.

Getting It All Together

I've told you everything I'm going to tell you about winemaking here. Any more would make a book on the subject, and there are several on the market already. So rather than give any new information in this section, what I'll do is describe the steps I went through in making two of my wines, so you can see where everything I've said so far fits in. It's the best way I can think of for ending my discussion of home winemaking.

The first wine whose making I'll describe is strawberry. Greer had been to a pick-your-own strawberry farm and had returned with fourteen quarts. She said I could have some for wine. I decided to make a gallon or so of sweet wine with a distinct strawberry flavor. I decided, rather arbitrarily, to use five pounds of strawberries. These (we chose the ripest) were hulled, rinsed, and put in a two-gallon crock, mashed up, and one gallon of hot water was poured over them. The water and berries were stirred up and mushed about thoroughly.

After the mixture cooled a bit I measured the acid level using a testing kit. It measured about .4%. So I added enough acid blend to raise the level to .6%. (How much was worked out by trial and error.) Next I pulled out some juice with a gravy baster, filled a testing jar, and took a specific gravity reading with my hydrometer. It was 10 degrees. I had decided to try for a specific gravity of 110. This meant the specific gravity had to be raised 100 degrees. According to my graph, that took about 2 3/4 pounds of sugar per gallon. But I had what looked like about a gallon and a quarter of stuff, with the strawberries included, so I guessed I would need somewhere in the neighborhood of 2 3/4 plus one quarter of 2 3/4 pounds sugar, or roughly 3.6 pounds of sugar. This calculation was just to give me some idea of what I would need. It wouldn't be exact since strictly speaking the strawberries weren't liquid, so the chart didn't apply, and also since I had only estimated the volume, not measured it. So I added 2 1/2 pounds of sugar, took another hydrometer reading, then added another 1/2 pound of sugar, and so on.

As it turned out my estimate was pretty close. Three and a half pounds of sugar brought it to a specific gravity of 111 degrees.

Now according to Rule 2, this 3 1/2 pounds of added sugar increased the volume by 3 1/2 × 1 1/4 or about 4 1/2 cups, slightly over a quart. Therefore I had over one and a half gallons of stuff to ferment. I usually add two or three tablets of yeast nutrient per gallon, so for this mixture I crushed up four and stirred them in well.

Finally, when the mess had cooled to room temperature, I sprinkled in a package of all purpose wine yeast, put a plate over it, and set it aside on Greer's treadle sewing machine (we were getting pretty cramped for crock space).

The next day I stirred the mixture gently. Gently because the crock was rather full.

The following morning was the fourth of July. We were rushing around frantically getting ready to go to the firemen's parade. Finally we got everything into the car. It wouldn't start. I looked happily at the few drops of rain falling and remarked, "Maybe there won't be a parade anyway." Greer said nothing. We went inside the house to pace while my father came over with jumper cables. It was then we noticed the strawberry mixture trickling down the sides of the crock and onto Greer's sewing machine. Greer said something I will not quote. I scurried off to the cellar to fetch a five-gallon crock, washed it and transferred the strawberry mixture into it. It seemed much happier with the extra room, and the sewing machine cleaned up quite well. My father came and we started the car. We were in time for the parade. And it didn't rain after all. There must be more of a moral to this besides "use a large enough crock," but I can't think of one.

The strawberry mixture worked away for a week. It was stirred thoroughly every day. Then I siphoned the liquid off the berries and into bottles. I filled a gallon and a quart bottle. I put a fermentation lock on the gallon bottle and stoppered the quart bottle with cotton. That's where it's at now.

In about three months I'll siphon the wine off the sediment into another gallon bottle with a fermentation lock, topping it up with wine from the quart bottle. I'll taste it at that time and maybe add a little sugar, or dilute it with water. Probably I won't do anything though. Then sometime next summer, if it looks clear, I'll bottle it. That's strawberry wine.

The second wine whose making I'll describe is red currant. The reason I chose this one to describe is that no fruit was involved in what I did, unlike the strawberry wine above. Also, it gives some idea of how to use up leftovers.

Greer had been making currant jelly. She had gone through her usual process of juicing currants; she got three cups of currant juice from the berries she had, and now she was left with a pillowcase full of mashed currants (which had not been squeezed: she had dripped the juice out). She poured three cups of hot water over this mash, let it drip, and squeezed the bag in the wine press this time. This "second run" juice she gave me and told me to do something with it. I decided to make a dry wine.

First I measured the quantity of juice I had. It turned out to be two pints four ounces, or thirty-six ounces. Next I measured the acid level. It was high: 1.35%. I wanted it to be .6% so it had to be reduced by .75%. I decided to do this by adding water. I used the formula given in the section on acid. Percent of reduction divided by percent desired, in this case, is .75 divided by .6, or 1.25. Had I had a gallon of juice, I should have added 1.25 gallons of water. I had thirty-six ounces of juice, so I added 1.25×36, or 45 ounces of water, that is, 2 pints 13 ounces of water. I know this seems like a lot of water, but the currant flavor seemed strong, so I figured it could stand the dilution. I added the water, winding up with about five pints of diluted juice with an acid content of .6% (I measured it again to be sure).

Next I took a specific gravity reading; it was 6 degrees. I decided to make a dry wine, so I wanted a specific gravity of about 95. Thus the specific gravity needed to be raised by about 90 degrees. According to my graph, that called for adding about two and a half pounds of sugar to a gallon. I didn't have a gallon, I only had five pints. There are eight pints in a gallon, so I had five-eighths of a gallon, therefore I added 5/8 of 2 1/2 pounds of sugar. This works out to be twenty-five ounces, or one pound nine ounces. I added a little less than this and measured the specific gravity again. I had hit 95, so I left it there.

Next I crushed a Campden tablet and a yeast nutrient tablet and stirred them in. I also added pectin-enzyme, since Greer told me the juice had lots of pectin in it. Finally I sprinkled in a package of all purpose wine yeast, covered the crock (which was big enough this time) with a plastic bag, tied around the edges, and let it work for about a week. From here on the process was the same as for the strawberry wine.

Well, that's it. For neither wine did I follow a recipe. But, by measuring and tinkering appropriately, I should wind up with wines about like those I wanted. And even if I don't, I'll have something that will be drinkable. That's one of the advantages of winemaking. Most mistakes can be passed off as successes—just lie about what you meant to make.

Beer

All the wines I've discussed so far have been made from fruit or flowers. What about cereal grains? The main difficulty is that most grains store energy in the form of starch, rather than sugar, so yeast has nothing to work on. Of course extra sugar can be added, and the grain used only for flavor. This is the principle of flower wines. But starch can make for a cloudy wine, and I suppose most people wouldn't much care for, say, a barley flavored wine.

There is, however, an enzyme which converts starch to sugar. One source of this enzyme is slightly sprouted barley seeds themselves. So, what could be done is this: take barley, let it just begin to sprout. This is called malting. Stop this sprouting, or malting, by roasting the grain. Crush up the malted barley, mix it with water, add yeast and let it ferment. The result historically is ale, a drink about a quarter to half the alcoholic strength of wine. Generally speaking, whether a dark or a light ale is produced depends on how much roasting the malted barley got.

Often this brew is flavored, and some centuries ago hops were generally settled on as a standard flavoring. This gives a bitter, refreshing taste, and acts as a preservative, which is important because of the low alcohol content of ale as compared with wine. With hops added, you have beer. These days, though, most ales have hops added too. The distinction between beer and ale has become rather fuzzy.

Finally, the beer can be put into bottles just before fermentation has finished. A little fermentation will go on in the bottles and the carbon dioxide produced will go into solution since the bottles are sealed. When the bottles are opened the beer will bubble and form a head of foam.

Since there is more enzyme produced by the malting of barley than is needed for the barley itself, these days most brewers add more starch to "stretch" the malt. This makes for cheaper beer without changing the taste greatly. Corn and rice are often used for this purpose.

Well, that's beer making. I think it's clear that not many people would carry it on at home using home-produced ingredients. Few people grow barley or hops, and the malting of barley is not simple. So most home brewed beers will be made from store-bought supplies. This puts home beer making in a different category from home winemaking. As a result, I'll just discuss the making of the simplest of homemade beers. If you want to get more deeply into the subject, there are several good books available.

After barley is malted, the malt can be removed as *malt extract.* You are familiar with this in malted milks, for example. For brewing purposes, malt extract can be had hop flavored, generally as a canned syrup. This is ideal for beginners, since nearly all the complicated work has been done. It's also good to use in bread baking, by the way. It is available at winemaking supply stores (and a few grocery stores) in cans ranging from two to three pounds. Much of it is British, but some American brands are available. Also, it is available in light, medium and dark, for beers of those qualities, and even for stout. There are generally recipes on the imported cans which call for nothing except the extract, water and yeast. But the recipe can be "stretched" by using extra sugar. So here's an all purpose basic recipe for doing that.

BASIC BEER RECIPE

1 can hop-flavored malt extract (2 – 3 pounds)	5 gallons water
2 – 4 pounds sugar	1 yeast packet

Boil as much of the water as you conveniently can. When it is boiling, stir in the malt extract. When it is mixed in (hot water helps get it out of the can) stir in the sugar, *except for five ounces* (withold one ounce per gallon). Then dump the liquid in a crock and add the rest of the water. When it has cooled to 65°–70°F (which may take overnight) add the yeast. Tie a plastic sheet or bag over the crock and leave it.

After a week siphon the liquid into a five-gallon bottle

and close it with a fermentation lock (leave a few inches of space between the liquid and the fermentation lock). Put any extra liquid in a smaller bottle, of course, and with a fermentation lock or cotton. The secondary fermentor can go in the basement, it needn't be kept warm.

After several weeks, depending on temperature and things, the beer will stop working and turn clear. After this happens (and don't be in a hurry, the beer is aging), siphon it off the sediment, out of the bottle back into a crock. Take out a little liquid, heat it gently, dissolve in it that five ounces of sugar you saved (it is dissolved when the liquid turns clear), and return it to the crock. Stir well, then bottle the beer in good beer or soda bottles, and cap *(not cork)* securely. Leave the bottles standing upright to age for a few weeks. A few months will be better. More fermentation will occur, this time in the bottle, making the beer fizzy. This produces a thin layer of sediment on the bottom of the bottles, so don't shake them. Also be careful when you pour the beer not to disturb the sediment. Stop pouring just before you reach it.

Well, that's the basic recipe. Now come comments. First, what was said about chlorine detergent for winemaking goes here too. The bottling techniques are the same, except don't use corks.

Use light hopped malt extract for light beers, medium for medium, dark for dark.

If the head is not enough, try bottling with six or seven ounces of sugar instead of five.

The recipe calls for sugar. Store-bought cane sugar will do, but it may leave a sour taste. Corn sugar is chemically somewhat different from cane sugar, and doesn't do this. Corn sugar is available at winemakers' supply stores, and costs only a little more than cane sugar. It is well worth it.

Baker's yeast will do, but it is not the best thing. Neither are wine yeasts. You'll be best off with an all purpose beer yeast, also available at winemakers' supply stores. If you get further into this, you will find there is as great a variety of brewing yeasts available as wine yeasts, each with different characteristics and tastes.

The general recipe above is vague about amounts. This is because tastes vary. The general principles are these: more malt extract makes for more body, and also more alcohol. More sugar makes for more alcohol but doesn't affect body. So, for example, if you like a strong-bodied but not strong beer, try two 2-pound cans of malt extract, but little sugar. Remember beer isn't meant to be a strong drink. A highly alcoholic beer just isn't beer.

If you have a hydrometer on hand for winemaking, you'll find it of use for beer making too. Specific gravity at the beginning should be somewhere between 30 and 45 for most brews. Here's a chart you can use as a rough guide.

QUALITY	SPECIFIC GRAVITY	% ALCOHOL
	30 – – – – – – –	3.7
mild – – – –		
	35 – – – – – – –	4.4
medium – – –		
	40 – – – – – – –	5.1
strong – – – –		
	45 – – – – – – –	5.8

So, select the alcohol strength you want, and aim at the corresponding specific gravity. Add enough hopped malt extract to get the body and flavor you want, then sugar to reach the proper specific gravity. Keep records and you'll soon hit the right recipes for you.

Also a hydrometer reading of about 1.000 means your beer is done working. Wine ends up a little below 1.000, but beer will finish a little above.

If you want to really get into home brewing, you'll soon

find there are lots of kinds of malted barley available besides extracts; and there are dried hops, and hop extract, and brewing salts, and water hardeners, and heading liquid, all kinds of things. You can work exclusively with traditional methods, using malted barley itself, or with a mixture of malted barley and malt extract. All kinds of combinations are possible. And they produce more kinds of beer than you ever dreamed of, most of them good. But I've said enough to get you started, and that's plenty for now.

Weights and Measures and Statutes

One of the truly infuriating facts of life for a home wine-maker is that there is no world standard for anything. The most dramatic of these disagreements is that both the United States and Great Britain use the word gallon for a measure of liquids, but they mean different things by it. Six U.S. gallons are five British gallons. Consequently, when following a recipe it is necessary to know where it came from, and this is not always easy to determine. Fortunately, the pound, as a weight standard, is the same. (Although French recipes are in grams.) Here is a conversion chart for adapting recipes. In it, the British and Canadian gallons, which are the same, are called Imperial gallons, the United States gallon is called a U.S. gallon (it is what we've used throughout this book).

If you are in the U.S., reading a British or Canadian recipe; either (1) *increase* the water called for by one fifth (that is, 1 3/5 U.S. pints extra for each gallon) *or* (2) *decrease* the weights called for by one sixth (that is 2 2/3 ounces for each pound, in other words, use 13 1/3 ounces where the recipe calls for one pound).

If you are in Great Britain or Canada, reading a U.S. recipe, either (1) *decrease* the water called for by one sixth (that is 1 1/3 imperial pints for each gallon, in other words, use 6 2/3 Imperial pints where the recipe calls for 1 U.S. gallon) *or* (2) *increase* the weights called for by one fifth (that is, 3 1/5 ounces extra for each pound).

I should mention that you can ignore the whole business, and follow a recipe as written. It will produce a different result than the author intended, perhaps, but one which will probably be pretty good anyway. If you choose to adapt recipes, it will almost certainly be okay to round off to the nearest pint or ounce.

There are a few other non-standard standards I should discuss, involving the hydrometer, acid measurement, and temperature.

All my hydrometer discussion has been in terms of specific gravity, but other hydrometer scales are sometimes used. The most common of these in winemaking is the Balling or Brix scale. This gives the sugar content directly in terms of percentage of weight. Thus a reading of 10 Balling means that 10% of the weight of the solution is sugar. The tendency in amateur winemaking is to do everything in terms of specific gravity, so I've said nothing about the Balling scale. Also, most winemaking hydrometers on sale these days have both specific gravity and Balling scales side by side, as well as potential alcohol scales, so it is all available just in case. I should also mention that there are maybe a dozen or more special purpose hydrometer scales around, for particular industries. Hydrometers giving readings in these scales are useless to a winemaker. Get a winemaking hydrometer, it is best for what you want.

Now, about acid measurement. I said it was the custom to select one acid as a standard and act as if all other acids present had been converted to that one. This is fine, and simplifies things, it is just that different countries have settled on different standards. The U.S. and Canada use tartaric acid as the standard, so .6% acid means .6% tartaric, that is, the acid strength is what it would be if .6% of the juice were tartaric acid. But Great Britain takes citric acid as the measure, while France uses sulphuric. Thus, .6% acid means something quite different in France than in England. That's the way it is. It is possible, of course, to convert them from one standard to another, but I doubt if you'll ever need to. I just thought you should know about it.

Finally there is the business of temperature scales. I've used the Fahrenheit scale, standard in the U.S., Great Britain, and Canada. But scientists and most of the rest of the world use the Centigrade scale. Sometimes recipes are found in Centigrade terms. Conversion between scales is easy, though.

To convert from Centigrade to Fahrenheit: take the temperature in degrees Centigrade, multiply by 9/5 (or 1.8), add 32.

To convert from Fahrenheit to Centigrade, take the temperature in degrees Fahrenheit, subtract 32, multiply by 5/9 (or .555).

So much for international confusion. Now I should say something about the legal aspects of the subject, or domestic confusion. Alcohol has the power to cloud men's minds, and that power is most evident in legislation concerning alcohol.

In the United States it is legal to make up to two hundred gallons of wine tax-free at home provided that one is head of a family. I quote from the federal form: ". . . a person is considered to be the head of a family only if he exercises family control or responsibility over one or more individuals closely connected with him by blood relationship or relationship by marriage, or by adoption, and who are living with him in one household." "He" means "he or she," so there's no women's liberation problem here, but it does mean you almost certainly can't legally make wine if you are not married. It appears to mean that you can't make wine legally if you are a widower with grown children. Silly, isn't it? Further, even if you qualify to make wine you can't serve it to anyone outside your family. Gets sillier, doesn't it? And finally, even though beer is much weaker than wine, you can't make any legally under these provisions. Presumably you'd need some sort of brewery license, and there'd be all sorts of massive taxes. So much for the wit and wisdom of the federal government. Oh, and there may be state regulations too.

If you want to make wine in the U.S. and you want to be law abiding, write to the Department of the Treasury, Bureau of Alcohol, Tobacco and Firearms, Washington, D.C. 20226 for form 1541 before you start. Fill out two copies and send them to the Assistant Regional Commissioner for your region. You must keep it available for inspection. And you must do this every year!

If you want to make beer in the U.S., you'll have to take your chances. I imagine they're pretty good. I've seen beer making kits on sale at major department stores around here. Somebody must be making the stuff, I suppose.

Finally, I strongly urge you to write your Congressman or Senator about this. It isn't good government to forbid the harmless.

If you live in Great Britain, the situation is more sensible. Since 1963, home beer making has been in the same category as home winemaking. I understand the situation is similar in Canada. Come on, us U.S.'ers, let's get our legislation in line with Canada's and Britain's (and also in line with what is probably the practice here anyway!).

Making Your Own Vinegar
Greer speaking

Mel said that vinegar-producing bacteria are around in the air. If you leave wine or beer open to the air in warm

weather for a few weeks it will vinegar. It will vinegar more
quickly if you put it into an uncovered crock or wide-
mouthed bottle (not over two-thirds full—put cheesecloth
over it to keep out flies), and stir it or shake it once a day. The
wine or beer should be completely finished working, because
once the vinegaring starts, alcohol production stops. The solution will vinegar even more quickly if you put a starter or
"mother" of vinegar in. This is hard to come by these days,
because store-bought vinegar is almost inevitably pasteurized, and the vinegar producing bacteria are killed off. Some
country stores, however, sell old-fashioned vinegar which has
not been pasteurized. If you can get some of this, and find a
sort of cloudy jellyish streak in it, that's the "mother" or
vinegar starter. Add it to the alcohol you are vinegaring. If
your unpasteurized vinegar doesn't have a mother, just add
some of the liquid. It probably contains some vinegar bacteria which will be happy to start working on your stuff. So
the recipe becomes:

HOMEMADE VINEGAR

**Dregs from dry wine, or from beer,
    or stale wine or beer
A dash of unpasteurized vinegar; or mother from unpasteurized vinegar (optional)**

Combine dregs from dry wine or beer which has finished
working. Fill a wide mouth bottle or crock not more than
two-thirds full, put cheesecloth over the top, and leave exposed to the air in a warm place. Shake or stir once a day for
best results. Let set for about six weeks in hot weather, longer
in cold weather, or until it is strong enough. (The traditional
place is the front porch. I often use the top of my refrigerator:
heat rises, remember. In back of the cookstove is another
traditional place which works well.) You may continue adding dregs to a brew which is vinegaring, but stop doing this

a couple of weeks before you want to use it. Siphon it off the sediment, strain it and bottle it for immediate use. You may, if you wish, bring it to a boil, then pack it into hot jars which will seal, but this is not necessary. If you don't do this, the vinegar may just continue working and getting stronger.

Reserve either the mother of vinegar or a sample of the vinegar to add to the next batch. You may vinegar cider the same way. By the way, my own taste is never to use the same bottles, crocks, or siphons for vinegar that you use for wines, just in case you don't wash them thoroughly enough. This is *particularly* the case if you happen to use barrels! The vinegar bacteria seeps into the wood and will work on anything alcoholic you see fit to put in it! By the way, my instructions said use *dry* wine to make wine vinegar: if you use sweet wine, you'll end up with sweet vinegar, unless you dilute the sweet wine and referment it into a dry wine before you vinegar it.

You may use homemade vinegar in cooking, in salads, mayonnaise or the like. But unless you can determine the acidity of your homemade vinegar, don't use it for pickling. You must have a vinegar of over 4% acidity for pickling. Most likely your homemade vinegar will get even stronger than store-bought vinegars (they are diluted for table use: read the label). But if it is way too strong, it will affect the taste of your final product; you'll want to dilute it. Faced with this problem with respect to my own homemade vinegars, I turned to Mel, and he worked out a method of testing for acidity.

Testing the Strength of Homemade Vinegar
Mel speaking

Here's a technique I've worked out for measuring the strength of homemade vinegar, using acid testing kits made for home winemakers. These are available from Sears Roe-buck and from winemakers' supply stores.

What can be done is this. Use any acid testing kit for wine, but use it on your vinegar. Follow the instructions which come with the kit. This will produce a certain number. Multiply that number by .8, that is, eight *tenths*. The result is the acetic acid strength of your vinegar.

One difficulty with this is the fact that it will use up a lot of your wine testing kit, since acid strengths of vinegar are lots greater than those of wine. So, in the interest of economy, here's a modified version of the above which will use up much less of your testing kit. Take a measured volume of your vinegar, and add to it nine equal volumes of water (thus diluting its strength by a factor of ten). I'd suggest you use the measuring device that comes with your wine testing kit do to this accurately. Now use your wine testing kit, following its instructions on this diluted vinegar. This will give you a number. Multiply it by what I will call our *magic number*, 8 (eight). The result is the acid strength of your vinegar.

A second difficulty is that winemaking kits are sometimes carelessly made, and may give inaccurate results. Also they may become inaccurate with age. Fortunately there's a way around this. Take some store-bought vinegar. Measure a quantity of it; dilute it with nine parts water, as above. Use your wine testing kit, following its instructions. The result will be a number. Divide that number into 5 if you had 5% vinegar, or into 4 if you had 4% vinegar (look on the label). The result is the magic number appropriate to your particular testing kit. Use it instead of 8 in the instructions of the last paragraph.

To reduce homemade vinegar that is too strong to 5%, add water as follows. Measure the acid strength; subtract 5;

divide the result by 5. Add that fraction of a gallon to each gallon of homemade vinegar. Also, if you want to reduce to 4% instead of 5%, subtract 4, then divide by 4, and proceed as above. That's all there is to it.

EPILOGUE: VISIONS

Greer and Mel speaking

Let us conclude this book with the vision we have for our place in about five years. We know our ideas may change. The very act of accomplishment changes what one desires to accomplish. And we have been changing lately, too. Still, we have some confidence in these plans. They have grown with us. We've watched them flesh out until now they seem solid enough to withstand any minor shifting on our part. We now know, or think we know, how, exactly, we want to live. Scarcely two years ago we could not have dreamed of this. Our concerns then involved things like cutting the lawn, or rather, having a lawn to cut. We had no idea what to do with most of our land, we hadn't even seen much of it. Now we know what we want on a grand scale, and we are making our land over to that end.

To begin with, we will have our spring garden and our big summer garden, and maybe scattered potato and corn

patches and a small grain field. These will supply all our
vegetables and flour. We have begun setting out fruit trees
and perennial beds. We plan to line a road with them, going
to a back field. That way, when they are big, we can drive
through with a wagon to fetch out fruit.

Just beyond the far end of the garden will stand our barn,
its front opening toward the state road, its back opening
toward a pasture. Upstairs will be a haymow, big enough to
let us feed our animals through the winter. Downstairs we'll
have the goats and sheep.

The goats should supply our milk needs. And with some
effort, our butter and cheese as well. We think we'll make
that effort. We already supply all our own wine and bread.
And there's the hen house. We supply all our own eggs now;
that will continue.

The sheep, of course, will supply us with spring lambs,
and give us a crop of wool to sell, or spin if it looks appealing.
At any rate, this will take care of some of our meat needs. We
might also try fattening up a calf from time to time. We'll see.

Just beyond the upper end of the garden, we'll have a
pond scooped out in what is now a swampy area. This will
give us water for the garden, and water for the livestock.
And, incidentally, a place for fish, ducks, and geese.

Stretching behind the barn, behind the garden, behind
the house, the full width of the property, will be a chain of
cleared fields, properly fenced, mostly pasture, a few planted
to corn or potatoes, one in berries. Things will be arranged
so that the sheep can go from the barn to the pasture by
themselves, if necessary, and water themselves at the pond,
too, in passing.

Behind the fields will be the forest, making up most of
the property. Properly managed, we should be able to harvest wood for all our cooking and heating, if we want, and
never make a dent in the supply.

Why all this? We're not quite sure. It seems to be the right thing for us. We're not saying it is morally right, or that everybody should do what we are doing. All we know is that it makes us happy.

Sometimes we muse over our dependence on organized society. We've been impressed by the extent of it. "Organized" is the key word. It is not enough that the country has petroleum, it needs refining and transportation to us before we can use it. And we do use it. But all it takes is a little perturbation in society and normal channels clog. "Things are tight," one is told. Well, if things get tight, are we really better off than we were in the city? We think so.

Come what may we can cook. We can heat. We have water (we put a hand pump on the well, just in case). We have vegetables. We have eggs, provided we can get or grow chicken feed. We will have meat, provided we can buy or grow hay for the winter, also milk, butter, and cheese. If worse really comes to worst, we could even manage pretty well without a car or tractor, but with a horse, provided we could buy or grow oats.

We don't expect we'll ever need a horse. But it is nice to know it's possible. It is one more option. We can heat with wood. Fine. We do have power failures, and fuel oil is getting scarce. We are not free of organized society. Nobody is. Even Thoreau borrowed an ax from Emerson, somebody made that ax, somebody sold it to Emerson. We are not free, nor should we be. But we are free of certain aberations of the corporate body common to the last quarter of the twentieth century. If we are not masters, at least we are not slaves. We are satisfied.

ANNOTATED
BIBLIOGRAPHY

Mel and Greer speaking

Here is a list of books we've found useful, together with some of our comments. We haven't made any systematic search—we expect there are many good books around we haven't seen—but we *use* these and can recommend them highly.

First we list books and pamphlet series of general use to a person moving to the country with plans for self-sufficient homesteading, then we give books grouped by subject matter, roughly following our chapter arrangement.

Here are the really basic, all-round books for all kinds of homesteading information. Two are older works, and one is British. They are all extraordinarily useful:

Five Acres and Independence, by M. G. Kains, Dover Publications, Inc., 1973 (reprint of 1940 edition) (paperback).

Living the Good Life, by Helen and Scott Nearing, Schocken Books, 1970 (first copyright 1954) (paperback).

Farming for Self-sufficiency, by John and Sally Seymour, Schocken Books, 1973 (first published in Great Britain) (hardbound).

A good book source for old-time country skills is *A Book of Country Things,* told by Walter Needham, recorded by Barrows Mussey, The Stephen Greene Press, 1965 (hardbound).

Akin to the above, but better known, are *The Foxfire Book* (1972) and *Foxfire 2* (1973), both edited by Eliot Wigginton, Doubleday (hardbound and paperback).

Used bookstores are good but unpredictable sources of homesteading information. Roughly speaking, good 1910 farming practices are just what the small self-sufficient farmer today should be following. Easily the most useful old work we've ever come across is this—if you ever see one, GET IT!!—*Farm Knowledge,* 4 volumes, edited by E. L. D. Seymour, prepared for Sears Roebuck by Doubleday, Page & Co, 1918.

Another old reference book, easier to come by in this area at least, is the following, which went through several different editions (the medical advice is generally dangerous, everything else is great): *Dr. Chase's Receipt Book and Household Physician, or Practical Knowledge for the People.* Our edition was published by F. B. Dickerson Co., in 1894.

By now many old editions of Sears Roebuck and Montgomery Ward catalogs have been reprinted. Many of them are inexpensive, and all of them are useful sources of information if you're trying to get a small farm going using methods of farming necessarily obsolete on the gigantic farms of today. Oh, and be sure to get the current Sears and Ward's catalogs. Whether or not you decide to buy from them, they provide you with information ranging from current chick prices to how to calculate the size furnace your house needs.

Countryside & Small Stock Journal, Rt. 1, Box 239, Waterloo, Wisconsin 53594. A great journal for the homesteader, with lots of practical advice on useful animals from rabbits to work horses.

The U.S. Department of Agriculture has an enormous list of useful, cheap or free publications. It is impossible to list all those which would be of use to the potential homesteader, so be sure and send for their catalog. Write to: Superintendent of Documents, U.S. Government Printing Office, Washington, D. C. 20402, and request the current "List of Available Publications of the United States Department of Agriculture." Enclose 45¢ (the list runs to 87 pages).

Every state in the U.S. maintains an Extension Service Program, which publishes a quantity of pamphlets on everything from pig raising and plumbing, to, at least in New York State, winemaking. The only one we are familiar with is New York State's. Its address is:

New York State Extension Service, Mailing Room, Bldg. 7, Research Park, Cornell University, Ithaca, New York 14850. Write for their catalog. They supply most of their publications to New York

State residents free, and to out-of-state people at a nominal cost. And write your own State Extension Agency. There is a list of addresses in *The Old Farmer's Almanack,* published by Yankee, Inc., and available on many country newsstands.

The Easi-bild people sell plans and instruction manuals for everything from houses to cradles. Write for their catalog to Easi-bild Pattern Company, Inc., Briarcliff Manor, New York 10510 (enclose $1.00).

A very sensible source of information is companies which manufacture materials and supplies homesteaders use. For example, the Pennwalt Corp., which manufactures several standard brands of lye among other things, will send on request detailed information on home uses for lye, including soap making, pretzels, hominy grits, tree sprays, quick compost making, etc. The address is Pennwalt Building, Three Parkway, Philadelphia Pa. 19102. Also try gelatin manufacturers, paraffin makers, canning supplies' manufacturers, etc.—use your imagination.

An unexpected source of good information is *Boy Scout Merit Badge Manuals,* some of which are on dairying, sheep raising, and the like. These manuals are carried by:

The Garden Way Publishing Company, Charlotte, Vermont 05445, and in addition, they carry a large supply of books and pamphlets on all things of interest to a homesteader. Their catalog costs $1.00, but the price will be credited to your first order. One of the book series Garden Way carries is the "Have-more" series. These are about the most useful reference works you can get. Typical item: a book, *Starting Right with Milk Goats;* others in the "Starting Right" series cover chickens, turkeys, sheep—you name it, there's probably a volume devoted to it. Closely related is a series of pamphlets by the same editors, Ed and Carolyn Robinson. Typical title: "Practical Hay-Making on a Small Place." These works are twenty-five years old, and were the bible of the last generation of homesteaders. They are as useful now as they ever were.

Speaking of publishers, get on Dover's mailing list (drop them a card). This reprint house has a most remarkable selection of books. Write Dover Publications, Inc., 180 Varick Street, New York, New York 10014.

This ends our list of general references. Now specific books:

Buying Country Property, by Irving Price, Harper and Row, 1972 (hardbound and paperback).

Restoring Junk, by Suzanne Beedell, Lancer Books, 1970 (paperback).

Knots, Useful and Ornamental, by George Russell Shaw, Bonanza Books, 1933 (hardbound). (Don't let the date fool you. It's been reissued.)

For information on building, rebuilding, wiring, plumbing and the like, one good source is the U.S. Department of Agriculture pamphlets and books. Another is the books and pamphlets available from Sears and Ward's (browse through their catalogs, you'll find several listed). The following books are *most* useful, almost indispensible. If you only plan to get one book, get this one:

Basic Construction Techniques for Houses and Small Buildings Simply Explained, prepared by the Bureau of Naval Personnel and republished by Dover Publications, Inc., 1972 (paperback).

A companion volume to the above, and extremely valuable, is:

Tools and Their Uses, prepared by the Bureau of Naval Personnel and republished by Dover in 1973 (paperback).

Wood-frame House Construction is a United States Department of Agriculture book (Handbook No. 73) available for $2.25 from the Superintendent of Documents, U.S. Government Printing Office, Washington D. C. 20402.

Build Your Own Low-cost Home is a Dover collection of eleven Department of Agriculture house plans in book form, together with a construction manual. The plans include specifications for materials down to the last nail. Dover Publications, 1972 (paperback).

A nice unofficial book to conclude the building section with is:

Making Do, by Arthur M. Hill, Ballantine Books, 1972 (paperback). Mr. Hill's ingenuity around the homestead is only matched by his clarity, and good sense.

We've tried out a number of tree identification books and were not satisfied with most of them. One that did prove useful, however, is:

Handbook of the Trees of New England, by Lorin L. Dame and Henry Brooks, Dover, 1972 (reprint of 1901 edition) (paperback). Comparable volumes are available for other parts of the country.

Before you start getting your orchard in shape, you might want to read these:

How to Prune Almost Everything, by John Philip Baumgardt, William Morrow and Co., Inc., 1968 (paperback).

The Grafter's Handbook, by R.J. Garner, Oxford University Press, 1967 (hardbound).

Less expensive than either of the above is a 25¢ pamphlet entitled:

"How to Prune and Trim," which we got from a manufacturer of pruning tools; Snap-Cut, Seymour Smith & Son, Inc., Oakville, Conn. 06779.

There are many good books on wild foods. The best known are those by Euell Gibbons, published by David McKay in both hardbound and paperback. We've found the following useful for us.

Stalking the Wild Asparagus, 1962.

Stalking the Healthful Herbs, 1966.

Stalking the Blue-eyed Scallop, 1964.

Any of his books will provide good entertainment and information. Other books useful in this connection are:

Edible Wild Plants, by Oliver Perry Medsger, Macmillan, 1966 (hardbound).

Edible Wild Plants of Eastern North America, by Merritt Lyndon Fernald and Alfred Charles Kinsey, revised by Reed C. Rollins, Harper and Row, 1958 (hardbound).

Feasting Free on Wild Edibles, by Branford Angier, Stackpole Books, 1972 (paperback).

Another resourse to tap is:

Maple Sirup Producers Manual, U.S. Department of Agriculture Handbook No. 134, available for $1.50 from Superintendent of Documents, U.S. Government Printing Office, Washington D. C. 20402.

If you raise sheep and process wool, the following may be useful (for the "how-to" of sheep and other livestock, see the "Starting Right with . . ." series listed above).

Dye Plants and Dyeing—A Handbook, Brooklyn Botanic Gardens (Brooklyn, N. Y. 11225) (paperback). (If you send for this, ask for a list of their other publications—many are useful.)

Natural Dyes and Home Dyeing, Rita J. Adrosko, Dover Publications, Inc., 1971 (paperback).

When you get your dairy started, be sure and get:

Making Homemade Cheeses and Butter, by Phyllis Hobson, Garden Way Publishing Company, 1973 (paperback).

An oddity involving another natural resource which will interest New Englanders and other mountain folk, at least, is:

The Forgotten Art of Building a Stone Wall, by Curtis P. Fields, Yankee, Inc., 1971 (paperback).

Since recreation is another natural resource your land can supply, active homesteaders in the snow belt will be interested in the following:

Complete Cross-country Skiing and Ski Touring, by William J. Lederer and Joe Pete Wilson, W. W. Norton and Co., 1970 (hardbound).

The New Cross-country Ski Book, by John Caldwell, The Stephen Greene Press, 1971 (paperback).

GARDENING: The two most useful organic gardening books we've found to date are the following: the first covers organic gardening in New England, the second in California. Both are entertaining and well worth reading.

Step By Step to Organic Vegetable Growing, by Samuel R. Ogden, Rodale Press, 1971 (hardbound).

Chico's Organic Gardening and Natural Living, by Frank (Chico) Bucaro and David Wallechinsky, J. B. Lippincott Co., 1972 (paperback).

The new gardener will find one or both of the following very useful:

Handbook on Biological Control of Plant Pests, Brooklyn Botanic Gardens, 1960 (paperback). Note: illustrated with photographs.

The Bug Book, Harmless Insect Controls, assembled by John and Helen Philbrick, 1963; write to the authors, P.O. Box 96, Wilkinsonville, Mass., 01590. (paperback). Note: Written with great verve and illustrated with drawings.

A somewhat more technical survey, though not as much use as a "how-to" for beginners, is:

Gardening without Poisons, by Beatrice Trum Hunter, Houghton Mifflin Co., 1971 (hardbound).

There are great numbers of weed books around. Our favorite is:

Selected Weeds of the United States, U.S. Department of Agriculture Handbook No. 366, write to Superintendent of Documents, U. S. Government Printing Office, Washington D. C. 20402 ($4.00) (paperback). This one is not only useful for the garden, but in the pasture as well, since it indicates plants poisonous to livestock.

And finally, home gardeners interested in "how to" may want to subscribe to:

Organic Gardening and Farming, Rodale Press, Inc., 33 East Minor Street, Emmaus, Penn. 18049 (a monthly magazine).

Once you are established and know how, if you are interested in information about starting an organic farming cooperative, try writing for information to:

National Sharecroppers Fund, 112 East 19th Street, New York, New York 10003. Also ask for their list of "Educational Materials Currently Available," which includes a newsletter issued bimonthly entitled *The Sharecropper,* and such pamphlets as "A Co-op Is Born." Try to enclose a donation large enough to cover at least printing and mailing costs, since this impressive organization works on a very tight budget.

Not directly useful as a "how to," but indirectly invaluable is:

Food in History, by Reay Tannahill, Stein and Day Publishers, 1973.

General Cookbooks: Here's what we consider the best all purpose cookbooks. They both give much valuable information on the standard food preservation techniques (canning, freezing, etc.).

Joy of Cooking, by Irma S. Rombauer and Marion Rombauer Becker, Bobbs-Merrill Co. We have the 1953 edition, but there are more recent ones (hardbound and paperback).

Just as useful is:

Fannie Farmer Cookbook, Bantam Books. This one too is revised every so often. We have the tenth edition (1970), revised by Wilma Lord Perkins (hardbound and paperback).

A good companion volume, which, among other things, explains the ins and outs of cooking with a coal stove, is:

The Original Fannie Farmer Cookbook 1896, a facsimilie of which was recently republished by Hugh Lauter Levin Assoc. (distributed by Crown Publishers) (hardbound).

We haven't said anything about baking bread in this book, but it certainly is a country art which can be easily a city or suburban one! Two books we learned from and still rely on are:

Bread—Making It the Natural Way, by Joan Wiener and Diana Collier, J. B. Lippincott Company, 1973 (hardbound).

Uncle John's Original Bread Book, by John Rahn Braué, Pyramid Books, 1961 (paperback).

Preserving Food for Winter: The most informative sources for canning and freezing recipes and information are the manuals which come with canners and are published by canning supply manufacturers. We rely most heavily on:

Ball Blue Book, Ball Corporation, Muncie, Indiana 47302 (enclose 50¢ for this instruction book which covers canning, freezing, pickling, and jell making).

The Modern Guide to Pressure Canning and Cooking, National Presto Industries, Inc. Write to Service Parts Dept., P.O. Box 10057, Northside Station, Jackson, Miss. 39206. The "part number" to order is 49563, and give the model pressure cooker you have. Enclose 50¢ plus 15¢ for postage and handling.

The second most useful source of canning, etc., information is the U. S. Department of Agriculture. If you want to pay for them bound into one volume, Dover has collected several pamphlets into book form:

Complete Guide to Home Canning, Preserving and Freezing, Dover, 1973 (paperback).

Or, you can get them as separate pamphlets free (one copy per person) by sending a post card to the Office of Information, U. S. Department of Agriculture, Washington, D. C. 20250. Ask for the following:

Home Canning of Fruits and Vegetables, G8
Home Freezing of Fruits and Vegetables, G10
How to Make Jellies, Jams and Preserves at Home, G56
Home Freezing of Poultry, G70
Making Pickles and Relishes at Home, G92
Freezing Meat and Fish in the Home, G93
Home Canning of Meat and Poultry, G106.

Not included in the Dover volume, but also of interest are:

Freezing Combination Main Dishes, G40
Storing Vegetables and Fruits, G119
Protecting Home-cured Meat from Insects, G109
How to Buy Meat for Your Freezer, G166.

By far the best all purpose book on food preservation techniques we've seen is:

Putting Food By, by Ruth Hertzberg, Beatrice Vaughan and Janet Greene, The Stephen Greene Press, 1973 (paperback).

A similar work, but more limited in scope (leaving out meat, soap, cheese, etc.) is:

Complete Book of Home Storage of Vegetables and Fruits, by Evelyn V. Loveday, Garden Way Publishing, 1972 (paperback).

For jelly and jam making, there are good recipe pamphlets with every box or bottle of Certo and Sure-Jell. Besides these, you can write for additional recipes which use these products: Write to:

Extra-special Jams and Jellies, Box 5067, Kankakee, Ill. 60901. Enclose 25¢.

Two delightful books on specialty preserving are:

Fine Preserving, by Catherine Plagemann, Simon and Schuster, 1967 (hardbound).

Old-time Pickling and Spicing Recipes, by Florence Brobeck, Gramercy Publishing Co., 1953 (hardbound).

A nice big omnibus style book, and very complete, is:

The Complete Book of Pickles and Relishes, by Leonard Louis Levinson, Hawthorn Books, Inc., 1965 (hardbound).

The Wine-Arts people, who run the most extensive chain of winemakers' supply stores, have produced two invaluable books for beginning winemakers:

The Art of Making Wine (1970) and *The Art of Making Beer*, (1971), both by Stanley F. Anderson with Raymond Hull. Hawthorn Books (hardbound and paperback).

A book equally as useful as the above is:

Guide to Better Wine and Beer Making for Beginners, by S. M. Tritton, Dover publications, 1969 (paperback). Indeed, any of Mrs. Tritton's works are recommended. Her book is British in origin, but no recipe conversion will be necessary for American readers as Mrs. Tritton has kindly given her recipes in British, American, and metric measures.

How To Make Wines and Cordials, by André L. Simon is an extensive collection of recipes from Old English Recipe books. Dover publications, Inc., 1972 (paperback).

Cornell University in New York State publishes worthwhile pamphlets on home grape winemaking and grape growing.

A very entertaining book on beer making is:

The Homemade Beer Book, by Vrest Orton, Charles E. Tuttle Co., 1973 (paperback), best obtained from The Vermont Country Store (see suppliers list to follow). The book is the proceedings of a literate bunch of home beer makers during prohibition. Mr. Orton is the last survivor of what was a spirited group, in all senses of the word.

Home Brewed Beers and Stouts, by C. J. J. Berry, The Amateur Winemaker, North Croye, The Avenue, Andover, Hampshire, Great Britian, 1971 (paperback) is an excellent modern work on home brewing oriented to the British reader.

Beer, by Anthony H. Rose, *Scientific American,* June 1959, Vol. 200, pp. 90–100. A really informative article on the history and current practices of beer making. It will make a lot of the mystery clear.

For the more advanced winemaker: there is:

Progressive Winemaking, by Peter Duncan and Bryan Acton, also published by The Amateur Winemaker, 1971 (paperback).

And a book not specifically about home winemaking, but about wines in general, which will be of interest to the home winemaker, is:

Wine, an Introduction for Americans, by M. A. Amerine and V. L. Singleton, University of California Press, 1972 (paperback).

The best source for the above books is a winemakers' supply store.

Finally, a free pamphlet on many things using malt, from bread-baking to vinegar making, is available from Premier Malt Products, Inc., Milwaukee, Wisc. 53201.

Unfortunately out of print, but worth looking up in a library are the following:

Curing Meats, by Hinman, Schutt and Holley, Cornell Extension Bulletin #241 (1940).

Making the Most of Your Freezer, by Marie Armstrong Essipoff, Rinehart and Co., 1951 (hardbound). This is a delightfully unorthodox treatment of the art of freezing food, well interspersed with the author's experiences with raising chickens, goats, sheep, etc.

SOURCES
FOR
SUPPLIES

We do a lot of our shopping by mail. Here are some of the people we like to do business with.

MONTGOMERY WARD. Look in your phone book for the nearest store, the company seems to be regionally organized, with different areas having different catalogs. In the Northeast, the address is simply, Albany, N. Y. 12201.

SEARS ROEBUCK & COMPANY, Boston, Mass. 02215.

Don't forget to get Ward's and Sears' farm catalogs, and any of their other special purpose catalogs which will be of use to you. These are listed in their main catalog and must be requested specially.

For sturdy outdoor clothing, shoes and boots in particular, as well as backpacks, tents, etc., write for a catalog to L. L. BEAN, INC., Freeport, Maine 04032.

THE VERMONT COUNTRY STORE, for old-style tools like slaw cutters, apple peelers; good edibles like cheese, stone ground flour; and odd items like beer mugs and ice creepers, etc. Write for their catalog to Weston, Vermont 05161. Enclose 25¢.

For things like hand (or electric) grist mills, etc., write to:

SMITHFIELD IMPLEMENT COMPANY, 99 North Main, Smithfield, Utah 84321.

EDMUND SCIENTIFIC, for pumps, soil testing kits, lenses, transistors, and, in general, the damnedest collection of scientific surplus. Write them at 623 Edscorp Building, Barrington, N.J. 08007.

We get much of our chicken feed, seed, tools, etc., from AG-

WAY, a farm cooperative supply house with branches through the northeastern United States.

Our favorite mail-order seed companies are:

STOKES SEEDS, INC., Box 548, Buffalo, N. Y. 14240. Write for their catalog. This company sells seeds for many varieties of garden vegetables *not* chemically treated for organic gardeners. It also sells the usual selection of treated seeds. Its catalog is particularly gay and informative.

BURPEE SEEDS, Box 6929, Philadelphia, Pa. 19132.

STARK BROS., NURSERIES, Louisiana, Missouri 63353 is an excellent nursery dealing in fruit and shade trees, bushes, perennials, etc. Write for their catalog.

We are far from expert at identifying wild plants. One way out of this difficulty which we hope to try out soon is to order some from a nursery, set them out, and see what they look like at all stages of development. Write for catalogs for the following wild plant nurseries:

PUTNEY NURSERY, Putney, Vermont 05346

VICK'S WILDGARDENS, INC., Box 115, Gladwyne, Pa. 19035.

INDEX

Acetic acid, 120
Acid blend, 212
Acid measurement, 45, 227
Acid-testing kit, 45, 211–214, 231–233
Acidity of food in canning, 100–101
Acids. *See* Winemaking
Aging wine, 188
Ale. *See* Beer
Animals, 99, 240, 241
Apples, 122, 125, 129, 168, 170

Baby food, 108, 147
Bacteria
  food spoilage, 99–102, 119, 145, 177
  in composting, 42, 50–52
  nitrogen-fixing, 40
Bail, 115

Basic beer recipe, 223
Basic flower wine recipe, 182–183
Basic fruit wine recipe, 197
Basic red wine recipe, 205–206
Basic store-bought fruit juice wine recipe, 197
Basic sugar wine recipe, 177–178
Basic white wine recipe, 207–208
Beans, 38, 40, 55, 58, 73–75, 157
Beer, 221–226, 247–248
Beef. *See* Meat
Beets, 57, 60, 68–70, 88, 166
Berries, 18, 20–22, 96, 122, 125, 128–131, 149, 196–198, 218–221. *See also* Jellies and jams; Winemaking
Birds, 37–39, 43
Black plastic mulch, 40